THE INQ
WE ASK THE QUE...

Mike Lewis
Rob Lewis
Mo Lewis

THE INQUIZITORS

We have raided our archive of quizzes from the past 30 years to produce a book of 10 question quiz rounds – and more - to suit any quiz event. We encourage readers who have purchased this book to use the questions and answers within the book for quizzing at home, online or as part of any quizzes presented for various social or fund-raising events. However, please do not use the illustrations. The licence to publish this book, in whole or part, remains with MRM and the copyrighted authors Mike, Rob & Mo Lewis. Enjoy!

DEDICATIONS

Mike: To Kath, Sam, Steve, Carole, Chris and all the other generous people who have helped us run our quizzes during the past 25 years or so. I am most grateful.

Rob: To Kate for putting up with all the hours spent on the laptop over the years and to Sam and Katie – the next generation of Inquizitors!

Mo: To my Dad, Wilfred, with love. I have missed you for so much of my life.

From all of us: If you have attended any of our quizzes and been complimentary - thank you very much. If you haven't enjoyed them - be assured we did our best!

Email: inquizitors3@gmail.com

ANSWERS TO EACH ROUND APPEAR AT THE BOTTOM OF THE SAME PAGE TO MAKE QUIZ SETTING AND TESTING EASY.

The black and white pictures throughout the book may provide some help with one answer in the relevant round.

The Inquizitors are: Mike Lewis, the founder, quiz writer and presenter. Rob Lewis, the techno man, vital to our multi-media quizzes, and the main presenter. Mo Lewis, arguably the most important member of the trio on quiz nights - the adjudicator. The Inquizitors were formed back in the 1990s and have clocked up hundreds of various sized quizzes. From small gatherings in church halls and pubs to huge venues such as Celtic Manor Resort, various Hilton Hotels, The National Museum, Cardiff, Gloucestershire Cricket Club and numerous football clubs including Bristol City, Bristol Rovers, Exeter City and Mangotsfield United. We have presented quizzes for charities and for corporate events as well as numerous organisations. Nowadays we tend to write more and perform less!

If you are thinking of running a quiz for the first time - pick the right venue! We always include both audio and video questions to add dimensions to the event. In fact, we present all our quizzes on PowerPoint. A half-time break should be included, with food it's even better. Sometimes The Inquizitors have hosted quizzes after B-B-Qs or meals.

Normally a quiz comprises between 50 and 100 questions and 6 to 10 rounds. That will take from an hour and a half to two and a half hours, so think carefully about what you require. There are many topics to choose from when creating rounds. Frequently specialised questions can be included. These are usually about employees, members, or companies and organisations. In addition to normal quiz questions The Inquizitors have included 'fun' rounds. Horse Racing on video, Food Taste, Team-building challenges and valuation of Antiques are just a few ideas.

Playing a Joker to double points for a selected round is the most popular. For charity events the Joker can be sold for, say £10, as an extra fund-raiser. Table Rounds are usually played during the half-time break and keep the quiz flavour going whilst the food is being enjoyed. This round is usually a series of pictures or questions on a printed sheet. Gamble Rounds involve attempting to identify an item from various clues. The quicker the answer is guessed the more points are earned. Of course, if the guess is wrong, no points are awarded and no further opportunity to guess is given.

There are a further three quiz books available on Amazon: *Quiz Encounters of the Trivia Kind: Quiz Builder*, *The Couch Potatoes Galaxy of British TV Quizzes* and *The Popcorn Munchers ABC of Film Quizzes*.

This book is dedicated to the many friends and acquaintances we lost during the pandemic. R.I.P.

INDEX

INDEX

THE INQUIZITORS

Pre-show!

5

JUST FOR STARTERS

Some easier one word answers to get you going!

1. The average person does what 13 times a day?

2. In cockney rhyming slang, what is a 'dog and bone'?

3. Which planet is closest to the sun?

4. What nut should you find in the middle of a Ferrero Rocher?

5. Name any one of the 14 landlocked countries in Europe.

6. An act of speaking against religion called what?

7. What us state contains the letter Z in its name?

8. As part of his formal investiture as Prince of Wales, in which Welsh town did a young Prince Charles study the Welsh history and language?

9. What colour are the seats in the House of Commons?

10. The ..... had a 1965 No.1 hit with Bob Dylan's *Mr. Tambourine Man*?

TV SIT-COMS

Hopefully to raise another smile or two!

1, What was the name of the store in *Are You Being Served*?

2. In which Devon seaside town was Fawlty Towers set?

3. In which sit-com did Michael Crawford make his name?

4. Una Stubbs died in August 2021, in what TV show did she play Rita Rawlins?

5. Who played Wolfie Smith, self-proclaimed leader of the Tooting Popular Front?

6. *Time On Our Hands* was the most watched episode of which major sit-com?

7. Fulton Mackay played a character with the same surname as himself in what?

8. Who wrote *Bread*, about a close-knit, working-class family in Liverpool?

9. What is the name of the cafe in Friends?

10. In which town is *The Office* set?

JUST FOR STARTERS ANSWERS: *1. LAUGH; 2. PHONE; 3. MERCURY; 4. HAZEL; 5. ANY ONE OF THESE! - Andorra, Austria, Belarus, Czech Republic, Hungary, Liechtenstein, Luxembourg, Macedonia, Moldova, San Marino, Serbia, Slovakia, Switzerland, and Vatican City; 6. BLASPHEMY; 7. ARIZONA; 8. ABERYSTWYTH; 9. GREEN; 10. BYRDS.* **TV SIT-COMS:** *1. GRACE BROTHERS; 2. TORQUAY; 3. SOME MOTHERS DO 'AVE 'EM; 4. TILL DEATH US DO PART; 5. ROBERT LINDSAY; 6. ONLY FOOLS AND HORSES; 7. PORRIDGE; 8. CARLA LANE; 9. CENTRAL PERK; 10. SLOUGH.*

THE YEAR 2021

1. In January 2021, on-line retailer Boohoo acquired which brand and website for £55 million?

2. Who was stung by criticism after it was thought her son Damian had taken pictures of her semi-naked in an open fur coat and bikini bottoms?

3. Captain Sir Tom Moore, sadly died at the age of 100. How many lengths of his garden did he walk to raise more than £32 million for NHS Charities Together?

4. Who won the second series of *The Masked Singer*?

5. On 9th April Buckingham Palace announced the death of the Duke of Edinburgh. How old was Prince Philip when he died?

6. What title does St Paul's Girls' School decide to drop, as it's 'too binary'?

7. Who was the famous former high profile owner of a Ford Escort, sold at auction for more than £52,000?

8. Weightlifter Laurel Hubbard was the first trans athlete to compete at the Olympics when she represented which country?

9. A new £50 banknote entered circulation on 23rd June, featuring which codebreaker's face on the reverse side to the Queen?

10. Police are called as protesters flock to Diddly Squat Farm - who is its famous owner?

Who was Henry VIIIs last wife?

IN THE YEAR 2020

What do you remember about this particular (or peculiar) year?

1. Which picturesque county Durham town caused a media frenzy for Dominic Cummings?

2. Which tennis player topped the 2020 Forbes magazine list of highest-paid athletes?

3. *You'll Never Walk Alone* was an April 2020 UK No 1 in honour of Captain Tom Moore. Which powerful male vocalist provided the vocals?

4. Who was Chancellor of the Exchequer during the Covid-19 lockdown?

5. Will Smith and which other main star reprise their roles in 'Bad Boys for Life'?

6. Best known for the song *Stay with Me*, which English singer released *To Die For* in 2020?

7. Which actor plays Dr Ivo Robotnik in the *Sonic the Hedgehog* movie?

8. An aeroplane on a commercial flight was 'unintentionally' shot down in Iran in January 2020, killing all 176 passengers and crew. Where had it flown from?

9. *Stupid Love* was the debut single from the album *Chromatica* from which US superstar?
a) Lady Gaga b) Britney Spears c) Madonna

10. *Gisaengchung* is the original title of this South Korean film which collected four Oscars in 2020. What is the English title?

IT'S A GAMBLE!

The quicker that you name the rock band, the more points you get!

5 POINTS. This band formed in 1971.
Signed for Asylum Records.
Released debut album 1972.

4 POINTS. Originally a 4-piece band.
Were Linda Ronstadt's backing band.
Added a fifth member.

3 POINTS. Hit albums include On the Border and The Long Run.

2 POINTS. Band members enjoyed solo success including Joe
Walsh, Don Henley and Glenn Frey.

1 POINT. Band named after a bird of prey who had a
worldwide smash with Hotel California.

NUMBER 2 HITS OF THE 1960s

10 hits to peak at No. 2 in the UK in the 1960s. Match the song to the artiste

1. EVERYBODY KNOWS	A. BOBBY DARIN
2. OH WELL	B. VIKKI CARR
3. MY BOY LOLLIPOP	C. BRUCE CHANNEL
4. IT MUST BE HIM	D. DAVE CLARK 5
5. LAZY RIVER	E. MILLIE
6. HEY! BABY	F. CLIFF RICHARD
7. IT'S ALL IN THE GAME	G. JOHN LEYTON
8. DOWNTOWN	H. BILLY FURY
9. WILD WIND	I. FLEETWOOD MAC
10. JEALOUSY	J. PETULA CLARK

ANSWERS - IT'S A GAMBLE: *THE EAGLES.*
NUMBER 2 HITS OF THE 1960s: *1D, 2I, 3E, 4B, 5A, 6C, 7F, 8J, 9G, 10H.*

FIND THE LINK

Four pictures. Find a connection!!

SPORTING CHANCE

1. What piece of fruit is found at the top of the Wimbledon Men's Singles trophy?

2. What are the 5 colours of the Olympic rings?

3. Who won the FIFA Women's World Cup in 2019?

4. How many world titles has Phil Taylor won in darts?

5. In football, which team has won the Champions League (formerly the European Cup) the most times?

6. In golf, where is the Masters played?

7. Which horse is the only three-time winner of the Grand National?

8. Since 1977, where is the venue for snooker's World Championship?

9. In bowling, what is the term given for three consecutive strikes?

10. Jade Jones took home gold for Team GB in the 2012 and 2016 Olympics. In what sport does she compete?

LETTER COUNTRIES

There are 11 countries in the World with 4-letter English names. Earn 1 point for each and a bonus 5 points for naming all 11.

FIND THE LINK ANSWER: ROCK BANDS (Eagles, Hives, Jam, Queen).
SPORTING CHANCE ANSWERS: 1. PINEAPPLE; 2. BLUE, YELLOW, BLACK, GREEN, RED; 3. USA; 4. 16; 5. REAL MADRID (13); 6. AUGUSTA NATIONAL; 7. RED RUM; 8. CRUCIBLE THEATRE, SHEFFIELD; 9. A TURKEY; 10. TAEKWONDO

THE FIRST SHALL BE LAST 1

The last letters of the answer will be the first letters of answer 2 and so on

1. What word can describe something you eat, a poker payment or a golf shot?

2. What is the penultimate letter of the Greek alphabet?

3. What prefix can go before act, course, face or national and is also an Italian football team?

4. Which river rises in Switzerland, flows through Lake Geneva and runs through south eastern France?

5. What can be the lighting, sound, or scenery used in a play, film, or broadcast or something you intentionally do to shock people or attract their attention?

6. What is the second astrological sign in the zodiac, an earth sign represented by the bull?

7. What word means a cessation of movement?

8. What is the quality of being elegant, stylish or upper class; the nickname of Peterborough United F.C.?

9. Name the 2019 coming-of-age drama that follows the journey of an extraordinary young girl raised in the forest, as she evades the relentless pursuit of an off-book CIA agent.

10. What is an annual publication listing a set of forthcoming events for the next year called?

BIRDS OF A FEATHER

All the answers contain the name of a bird

1. Which famous architect designed St Paul's Cathedral?

2. What name is given to a score of 3 under par for a hole in golf?

3. What were the first four words broadcast from the surface of the moon?

4. Which Falkland Islands' airstrip did British troops recapture on 28 May 1982 during the Falklands conflict with Argentina?

5. In which country could you see the ruins of the ancient city of Ephesus?

6. Which 800 ft high building in London's Docklands was designed by Cesar Pelli?

7. Which song was a UK number one for Spitting Image?

8. Which town in South Bedfordshire stands at the north eastern end of the Vale of Aylesbury?

9. What was the name of Sleepy Hollow's schoolmaster in stories by Washington Irving?

10. Who "went to sea in a beautiful pea green boat"?

BIRDS OF A FEATHER ANSWERS: : 1. SIR CHRISTOPHER WREN; 2. AN ALBATROSS; 3. THE EAGLE HAS LANDED; 4. GOOSE GREEN; 5. TURKEY; 6. CANARY WHARF TOWER (ONE CANADA SQUARE); 7. THE CHICKEN SONG; 8. LEIGHTON BUZZARD; 9. ICHABOD CRANE; 10. THE OWL AND THE PUSSYCAT.

HAVE A DRINK ON ME

A round about liquid refreshment

1. What is Homer Simpson's favourite beer?

2. Which Irish company makes Baileys Irish Cream?

3. Cinzano dates from 1757. In which Italian city was the herbal shop that created the 'new' vermouth?

4. Who had a hit in 1961 with Have A Drink on Me?

5. With what is the Belgian beer Kriek flavoured?

6. By what name do the Brits call the light red wines of Bordeaux?

7. Which liqueur is made with whisky and heather honey?

8. If a quality cognac has been in the barrel for 5 and 8 years, how many golden stars would it be awarded?

9. In the French steak dish Tournedos Rossini which fortified wine is used to make the demi-glace sauce?

10. From which South American country does Tequila originate?

ANIMAL COLLECTIVES

By what names are groups of the 15 animals listed familiarly known?

1. MOLES

2. GIRAFFES

3. JAGUARS

4. PORCUPINES

5. WOMBATS

6. SLOTHS

7. LIONS

8. LEMURS

9. HEDGEHOGS

10. BADGERS

11. DOLPHINS

12. BATS

13. SEALS

14. BUDGERIGARS

15. COBRAS

ANIMAL COLLECTIVES ANSWERS: 1. LABOUR; 2. TOWER; 3. PROWL (OR SHADOW); 4. PRICKLE; 5. WISDOM; 6. BED (OR SNUGGLE); 7. PRIDE (OR SAWT); 8. CONSPIRACY; 9. ARRAY; 10. CETE; 11. POD; 12. COLONY (OR CAULDRON); 13. HAREM; 14. CHATTER; 15. QUIVER.

HIT SONG LYRICS

We give you the second line of the lyrics to 10 major UK hits, but what was the first line?
As an aid we give the year of issue and highest chart position the song reached.

1. Somehow I made it through. *(No. 3 in 1984)*

2. Me and Susie had so much fun. *(No. 2 in 1972)*

3. In her pretty cabinet. *(No. 2 in 1974)*

4. My heart's in overdrive and you're behind the steering wheel. *(No. 2 in 2003)*

5. One man come and go. *(No. 3 in 1984)*

6. I'm beggin' of you, please don't take my man. *(No. 7 in 1976)*

7. I'm punching my card. *(No. 6 in 1984)*

8. As long as stars are above you. *(No. 3 in 2013)*

9. But then I know it's growing strong *(No. 8 in 1971)*

10. Kept thinkin' I could never live without you by my side. *(No. 1 in 1979)*

HIT SONG LYRICS ANSWERS: *1. I made it through the wilderness - Like a Virgin (Madonna); 2. I remember when rock was young - Crocodile Rock (Elton John); 3. She keeps the Möet & Chandon - Killer Queen (Queen); 4. Can't explain all the feelings that you're making me feel - I Believe in a Thing Called Love (Darkness); 5. One man come in the name of love - Pride (In the Name of Love) (U2); 6. Jolene, Jolene, Jolene, Jolene - Jolene (Dolly Parton); 7. Been working so hard - Footloose (Kenny Loggins); 8. How long will I love you? - How Long Will I Love You? (Ellie Goulding); 9. Where it began, I can't begin to know when - Sweet Caroline (Neil Diamond); 10. At first I was afraid, I was petrified - I Will Survive (Gloria Gaynor).*

TAKE YOUR PICK

Just select A,B,C or D

1. What is a hippophobe afraid of?
A) Hippopotami   B) Fish   C) Horses   D) Theatres

2. In which year did the Japanese bomb Pearl Harbour?
A) 1939   B) 1940   C) 1941   D) 1942

3. In what stage show would you see Yum-Yum, Ko-Ko and Nanki-Poo?
A) Teletubbies Live   B) The Borstal Boy   C) The Mikado   D) Warhorse

4. What is the date of St George's Day?
A) 23rd April   B) 1st April   C) 17th April   D) 5th May

5. Who was the first Beatle to have a No.1 hit after the band disbanded?
A) John   B) George   C) Ringo   D) Paul

6. Where were the 2004 Olympic Games held?
A) Sydney   B) Beijing   C) Athens   D) Frankfurt

7. What does the name *Mississippi* mean?
A) Big river B) Muddy river C) Blood river D) Dry river

8. From which language is the word 'tattoo' taken?
A) Hindustani B) Tahitian C) French D) Arabic

9. Who is the victim in the original 1943 game of *Cluedo*?
A) Mr. Blue   B) Dr. Black   C) Mr. Brown   D) Mr. Pink

10. Who wrote the musical The Beautiful Game with Andrew Lloyd
Webber?   A) Mark Knopfler B) Ben Elton C) Elton John D) Tim Rice

TAKE YOUR PICK ANSWERS: 1. B) HORSES; 2. C) 1941; 3. C) THE MIKADO;
4. A) 23RD APRIL; 5. B) GEORGE (MY SWEET LORD); 6. C) ATHENS; 7. A) BIG
RIVER; 8. B) TAHITIAN; 9. B) DR BLACK; 10. B) BEN ELTON.

MAKE THE CONNECTION 1

4 PICTURES. What is the connection?

WHO AM I?

5 CLUES TO IDENTIFY A MUSIC LEGEND

1. **5 PTS.** Mystery lady was a famous name in music. Born Memphis in 1942.

2. **4 PTS.** Played a singing waitress in The Blues Brothers in 1980.

3. **3 PTS.** Hits include Spanish Harlem, I Say A Little Prayer, A Deeper Love.

4. **2 PTS.** Topped the charts in 1987, duetting with George Michael.

5. **1 POINT.** The Queen of Soul died, aged 76, in 2018.

TAYLOR SWIFT TOP 10

10 hits of Taylor's that reached different chart positions - match them up!

Chart Position	Song
1	A) Everything Has Changed
2	B) The 1
3	C) Me!
4	D) Exile
5	E) Look What You Made Me Do
6	F) I Don't Wanna Live Forever
7	G) Cardigan
8	H) Love Story
9	J) We Are Never Ever Getting Back Together
10	K) 22

MAKE THE CONNECTION ANSWERS: *All bigger on the inside than the outside!* **WHO AM I? ANSWERS:** *ARETHA FRANKLIN.* **TAYLOR SWIFT TOP 10 ANSWERS:** *1E, 2H, 3C, 4J, 5F, 6G, 7A, 8D, 9K, 10B.*

TRUE OR FALSE?

One or the other!

1. In *Close Encounters of the Third Kind*, mashed potato is sculpted into a plateau?

2. The White House, Washington DC has 2,000 rooms?

3. Friday the 13ths only occur whenever a month starts with a Sunday?

4. Cows have half a dozen stomachs?

5. Ants sleep 16 hours a day?

6. Letters in Braille are referred to as cells?

7. You share your birthday with over 9 million people worldwide?

8. Robert Wrigley created the first chewing gum?

9. The bodies of dead workers are buried in the Hoover Dam?

10. Sweden fuels its transportation system using smuggled booze?

5-4-3-2-1

The quicker you identify him the more points you score!

1. 5 POINTS This man was born Grigori Effimovich in 1869 and died in 1916.

2. 4 POINTS. Portrayed in films by Christopher Lee and Alan Rickman etc.

3. 3 POINTS. Died from drowning after surviving stabbing,

being shot, poisoned, battered and strangled.

4. 2 POINTS. Son of a peasant, joined a monastery at 16.

Powerful in The court of Czar Nicholas II.

5. 1 POINT. Nicknamed the Mad Monk.

His name was the title song of a Boney M No. 2 in 1978.

TRUE OR FALSE? ANSWERS: 1.TRUE; 2. FALSE; 3.TRUE; 4. FALSE; 5. FALSE; 6.TRUE; 7.TRUE; 8. FALSE; 9. FALSE; 10.TRUE.
5-4-3-2-1 ANSWER: GRIGORI RASPUTIN.

COMMERCIAL BREAK

Adverts on the Telly

NAME THE PRODUCTS THAT ARE BEING ADVERTISED

COMMERCIAL BREAK ANSWERS: *1. HOVIS; 2. LLOYDS BANK; 3. HAMLET CIGARS; 4. AMAZON ALEXA; 5. GO COMPARE; 6. O2; 7. McDONALD'S BIG MAC; 8. ALDI; 9. SEAT ATECA; 10. SONY BRAVIA.*

MUSIC QUEST

How well do you know your popular music?

1. How is controversial rapper Marshall Mathers better known?

2. Which song from Michael Jackson's *Thriller* album was the only UK No. 1?

3. What is the first word of Celine Dion's *My Heart Will Go On*?

4. What number was Perfect for the Beautiful South back in 1998?

5. Which singer recorded the 2002 chart-topping album *Come Away with Me*?

6. Which James Bond theme song did Tina Turner perform?

7. In which Wiltshire town was Eddie Cochran killed in 1960?

8. And what is the connection between Eddie Cochran's taxi driver and The Beatles record producer?

9. Who was the only Beatle to change his surname?

10. In which US state would you find Elvis Presley's mansion Gracelands?

M STATES OF THE US

List the eight states of America beginning with the letter M

MUSIC QUEST ANSWERS: 1. EMINEM; 2. BILLIE JEAN; 3. EVERY; 4. 10; 5. NORAH JONES; 6. GOLDENEYE; 7. CHIPPENHAM; 8. BOTH NAMED GEORGE MARTIN; 9. RINGO STARR (RICHARD 'RINGO' STARKEY; 10. TENNESSEE. M STATES OF AMERICA ANSWERS: MAINE, MARYLAND, MASSACHUSETTS, MICHIGAN, MINNESOTA, MISSISSIPPI, MISSOURI, MONTANA.

TESTING, TESTING!

A round about the various challenges of life!

1. What is the longest form of the game of cricket?

2. The MOT test was launched in 1960. At what age were vehicles initially required to be tested?

3. In education National Curriculum assessments are colloquially known as SATs. What does this acronym stand for?

4. The Ishihara test is used to test for which condition?

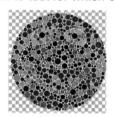

5. Where in the UK is the River Test, a 64 km (40 mile) river?

6. Which age group benefits from Apgar tests?

7. In chemistry what test is used to determine the acidity or alkalinity of a solution?

8. Carole Hersee appeared on BBC TV screens for 31 years as, what?

9. Trinity was the code name for the first testing of what?

10. In which year was the separate written theory test introduced as the first stage of obtaining a UK driving licence?

MISSING LINK - 1

Look at the 3 pictures and work out what should go in box 4

CORRACHADH MÒR	DUNNET HEAD	LOWESTOFT NESS	?

ANSWERS: 1. TEST CRICKET; 2. 10 YEARS; 3. STANDARD ASSESSMENTS TESTS, 4. COLOUR BLINDNESS; 5. HAMPSHIRE; 6. NEW-BORN BABIES, 7. LITLUS TEST; 8. THE TEST CARD GIRL; 9. ATOM BOMB, 10. 1996.
MISSING LINK - 1 ANSWER: *LIZARD POINT (Extreme points of British mainland).*

MULTI-CHOICE

Choose A, B, C, or D

1. Who is the only Scot to captain the England cricket team?
A) Mike Gatting   B) Mike Brearley   C) Mike Atherton   D) Mike Denness

2. What did William Blake want to build in England's green and pleasant land?   A) A better world   B) Britannia   C) A Supermarket   D) Jerusalem

3. What was the first ever breathalyser called?
A) Drunkometer   B) Sober-U-Up   C) Boozogauge   D) Slurry

4. Name the Roman god of agriculture, wine and fertility?
A) Dionysus   B) Timon   C) Liber   D) Bacchus

5. When was the postcode first introduced into the UK?
A) 1940   B) 1959   C) 1968   D) 1971

6. What is an axolotl?   A) A virus   B) Multi-axled vehicle   C) Type of mortice   D) Species of salamander

7. After Adam, Eve, Cain and Abel who is the next person mentioned in the Bible?
A) Enoch   B) Jubal   C) Lamech   D) Zillah

8. What is Johnny Depp afraid of?
A) Jugglers   B) Clowns   C) Ringmasters   D) Lion tamers

9. When Mt. St. Helens erupted on May 18, 1980, how many people were killed?   A) 27   B) 57   C) 87   D) 997

10. You're in third place right now in a race. What place are you in when you pass the person in second place?
A) 1st   B) 2nd   C) 3rd   D) 4th

**Which actress has played Emmerdale's
Mandy Dingle since 1995?**

FIND-THE-LINK

*Find the connection between all the correct answers **FOR A 5 POINT BONUS***

1. In motor racing, what colour flag orders a driver to return to the pits?

2. 'Rub-a-dub-dub, three men in a tub, the butcher, the baker and whom?

3. Which UK venue opened to the public in September 1867. Still the largest concert hall in Bristol, being refurbished and renamed in 2020.

4. What bird in some countries is also a symbol of pride or vanity, due to the way the bird struts and shows off its plumage?

5. What Beatles album originally included *Eleanor Rigby*, *Yellow Submarine* and *Taxman*?

6. Name the main research library of Oxford University — one of the oldest libraries in Europe, ?

7. Name the Claude 'Curly' Putnam country song first recorded by Johnny Darrell and subsequently by Porter Wagoner, Jerry Lee Lewis and Bobby Bare before being a UK number one hit for Tom Jones in 1966?

8. Nigel Slater, Lorraine Pascale and Madhur Jaffrey all appear on TV programmes centred upon which place of work?

9. Name the actress who starred in *The Avengers* in 2010 and *Match Point* in 2005, who also won a Tony Award for *A View from A Bridge* in 2010?

10. Name the comparatively soft, malleable bluish grey metal used for flushing on roofs.

Which US musician played Napster founder Sean Parker in the film The Social Network?

*FIND-THE-LINK ANSWERS: 1. BLACK; 2. THE CANDLESTICK MAKER; 3. THE COLSTON HALL; 4. PEACOCK; 5. REVOLVER; 6. BODLEIAN LIBRARY; 7. THE GREEN GREEN GRASS OF HOME; 8. THE KITCHEN; 9. SCARLETT JOHANSSON; 10. LEAD. **THE LINK IS THE GAME OF CLUEDO.** TRIVIAtime ANSWER: JUSTIN TIMBERLAKE.*

QUESTIONS OF SPORT

More fun and games

1. What is the largest capacity cricket ground in England?

2. In which sport do competitors refer to 'catching a crab'?

3. Complete the name of the current NBA champions: Toronto _____.

4. Who is the only player to have scored in the Premier League, Championship, League 1, League 2, Conference, FA Cup, League Cup, Football League Trophy, FA Trophy, Champions League, Europa League, Scottish Premier League, Scottish Cup and Scottish League Cup?

5. Coco Gauff made headlines at Wimbledon in 2019 when she beat Venus Williams. How old was she?

6. At which Olympics did Kelly Holmes win two gold medals?

7. After retiring from professional cycling, in what other sport did Bradley Wiggins briefly attempt to make a career?

8. In which outdoor sport would you need a stick, a puck and a mouth guard?

9. In rugby union, who is England Men's all-time top try scorer?

10. Who is the Premier League's all-time top scorer?

ADORER MOTLEY is a TV presenter in anagram form. Can you name her?

QUESTIONS OF SPORT ANSWERS: 1. LORDS; 2. ROWING; 3. RAPTORS; 4. GARY HOOPER; 5. 15; 6. 2004 – ATHENS; 7. ROWING; 8. HOCKEY; 9. RORY UNDERWOOD; 10. ALAN SHEARER. TRIVIAtime ANSWER: HELEN SKELTON.

FIRSTS

All types of originals

1. Which British bank was the first to issue cash dispenser cards?

2. According to the Bible, who was first to see Jesus after his resurrection?

3. Who was the first woman to read the news on television?

4. Which support group was founded in Ohio in 1935?

5. What was first revealed at Lords during a cricket match in 1975?

6. Which famous first in TV advertising is held by *Bird's Eye Frozen Peas*?

7. What first did Cathy Sullivan achieve in 1984?

8. In 1714 Henry Mill was granted the first patent for which machine?

9. Who, in 1975, was the first black player to win the Wimbledon Singles title?

10. Joseph Mornier patented which building material?

NAME THE ARTIST

A cover of Vogue in 2020 – Wheat Field Near Fridaythorpe. Who painted it?

FIRSTS ANSWERS: *1. BARCLAYS; 2. MARY MAGDELENE; 3. ANGELA RIPPON; 4. ALCOHOLICS ANONYMOUS; 5. A STREAKER; 6. FIRST PRODUCT ADVERTISED ON COLOUR TV; 7. SHE WAS THE FIRST WOMAN TO WALK IN SPACE; 8. TYPEWRITER; 9. ARTHUR ASHE; 10. REINFORCED CONCRETE.*

TRIVIA TEST
How's your know how?

1. How many sides would a dozen dice have in total?

2. Who wrote the classic song I Will Always Love You?

3. What type of goat produces mohair?

4. Pigs are used to sniff out which delicacy?

5. In which Chinese city did the coronavirus allegedly start?

6. What is produced by the bacterial fermentation of milk?

7. What date in 2020 did the UK go into lockdown?

8. Glossectomy is the removal of all or part of which body part?

9. Which British explorer was murdered by the natives in Hawaii?

10. Which golfer was known as The Golden Bear?

DINGBAT
Can you solve these puzzles?

THE LAST SHALL BE FIRST

The last letter of answer 1 will be the first letter of answer 2 and so on

1. Name the south eastern US state, that stretches from the Chesapeake Bay to the Appalachian Mountains, with a long Atlantic coastline.

2. What is a sparkling white Italian wine that is produced throughout south eastern Piedmont?

3. Name the knighted English actor whose career spans genres ranging from Shakespearean and modern theatre to popular fantasy and science fiction. Starred in Vicious and Lord of the Rings.

4. Who was the English centre-forward who died in 2011 and was nicknamed 'The Lion of Vienna'? (Both names)

5. Name the fast-growing evergreen tree, native to Australia. An ingredient in many products and the staple diet for koalas.

6. What is Russia's cultural centre, with venues such as the Mariinsky Theatre and the State Russian Museum?

7. What device invented by the Romans around 260 BC, also called a grappling hook, was originally used in naval warfare to catch ship rigging so that it could be boarded?

8. Who was one of the Knights of the Round Table in the Arthurian legend who features as King Arthur's greatest companion and the greatest swordsman and jouster?

9. What is the surname of the prime minister of the UK from 4 May 1979 – 28 November 1990?

10. Which twin was legendary founder and first king of Rome 753–716 BC?

TRIVIAtime

Starting with Heartbreak Hotel, how many consecutive US chart number 1s did Elvis Presley achieve?   A)7 B) 9 C) 11

THE LAST SHALL BE FIRST ANSWERS: 1. VIRGINIA; 2. ASTI; 3. IAN McKELLEN; 4. NAT LOFTHOUSE; 5. EUCALYPTUS; 6. ST. PETERSBURG; 7. GRAPNEL; 8. LANCELOT; 9. THATCHER; 10. ROMULUS. TRIVIAtime ANSWER: C) 11.

DOUBLE MEANINGS

Two descriptions, one word!

1. Which word describes sailors and medical minerals?
2. Which word can be a musical sound or a short letter?
3. Which word can describe a group of schoolchildren or a social category?
4. What part of a castle can also be a word meaning to retain?
5. Which word for lazy can also mean to tick over?
6. What part of cooked chicken might be used by a percussionist?
7. Which flatfish shares its name with a part of the foot?
8. What word can be payment for a journey or food?
9. What word can be a number or the outline of the body?
10. What word can be a sauce for salad or putting clothes on?

ICONIC INTERIORS

Can you identify the 3 BBC-TV sit-coms from these 3 empty sets?

DINGBATS
Can you solve these puzzles?

A

♂
BORED

B

B
E
D
W
CHARLES
R
D

C

WHERE

Frilly

SWEET SHOP

Can you recall these childhood favourites in the corner shop?

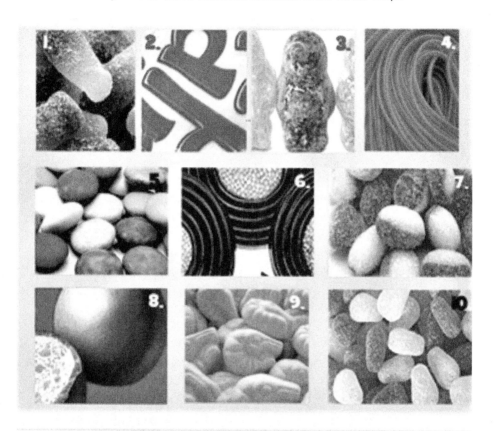

WHAT IS THIS SAYING?

SWEET SHOP ANSWERS: *1. COLA BOTTLES; 2. DIB DAB; 3. JELLY BABIES; 4. STRAWBERRY LACES; 5. SMARTIES; 6. LIQUORICE CATHERINE WHEELS; 7. RHUBARB AND CUSTARD; 8. MALTESERS; 9. SHRIMPS; 10. PEAR DROPS. WHAT IS THIS SAYING? ANSWER: EVERY DOG HAS ITS DAY.*

50 / 50 QUESTIONS

Easy pickings!

1. Who wrote Alexander's Ragtime Band – Cole Porter or Irving Berlin?

2. On which river would you find the Aswan High Dam – Nile or Zambezi?

3. What is most of the earth's surface covered by – desert or water?

4. Are Pentland Javelin and Desiree types of computer language or potato?

5. In Thailand do motorists drive on the right or left?

6. What colour car does the Pink Panther drive in the cartoons – pink or gold?

7. In darts what is the difference between the highest treble and the lowest treble scores – 49 or 57?

8. Does a hovercraft move along on a cushion of air or a cushion of water?

9. Which vegetable is produced from the plant maize – sweetcorn or lentils?

10. Agatha Christie wrote about The Murder of Roger … Ackroyd or Styles?

WHO'S TO BLAME?

Complete these hit song titles

A. Blame it on ………… (B*witched 1999)

B. Blame it on …… …… (The Jacksons 1978)

C. Blame it on …… …… …. (Eydie Gorme 1963)

D. Blame it on …. (D:Ream 1994)

50/50 QUESTIONS ANSWERS: *1. IRVING BERLIN; 2. NILE; 3. WATER; 4. POTATO; 5. LEFT; 6. PINK; 7. 57; 8. AIR; 9. SWEETCORN; 10. ACKROYD.* **WHO'S TO BLAME:** *A) THE WEATHERMAN; B) THE BOOGIE; C) THE BOSSA NOVA D) ME.*

PASS WITH FLYING COLOURS!

A colourful round

1. What is the largest airline in India by passengers carried and fleet size, with a 47.5% domestic market share as of November 2019?

2. In which TV series is the ship's computer called Holly?

3. Christie had a 1970 No.1 hit with which song rejected by The Tremeloes?

4. Who presented the original ITV version of the quiz *Double Your Money*?

5. Which university are the light blues?

6. The Orange River forms the southern border of which African country?

7. What TV show links Christopher Wenner, Katy Hill and John Leslie?

8. What is the more familiar name for the herbaceous flowering plant called Saintpaulis?

9. Which 2010 film starred Bruce Willis, Helen Mirren and Morgan Freeman?

10. 'Look at the stars, look how they shine for you'; are lyrics from which 2000 number 4 UK hit?

SPOT THE MOVIE!

Film titles in picture form

  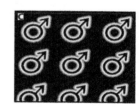

PASS WITH FLYING COLOURS ANSWERS: 1; INDIGO; 2. RED DWARF; 3. YELLOW RIVER; 4. HUGHIE GREEN; 5. CAMBRIDGE; 6. NAMIBIA; 7. BLUE PETER; 8. AFRICAN VIOLET; 9. RED; 10. YELLOW (Coldplay). SPOT THE MOVIE! ANSWERS: A) THE SILENCE OF THE LAMBS; B) RAMBO; C) MEN IN BLACK.

CLASSICAL GAS

Who composed these well-known pieces of classical music?

1. Rhapsody in Blue
2. Ode to Joy
3. The Hallelujah Chorus
4. The 1812 Overture
5. The Lark Ascending
6. Nessun Dorma
7. Land of Hope and Glory (Pomp and Circumstance)

8. Bolero
9. The Wedding March (in C Major)
10. Air on the G String

MISSING VOWELS

Various things people say when shaking hands – with the vowels removed!

1. H WD YD
2. PLS DT MT Y
3. WL LPL YD
4. C NG RTL TNS
5. HR DL CK

Abel Makkonen Tesfaye is the stage name of which act who released 'Blinding Lights' in 2020?

CLASSICAL GAS ANSWERS: *1. GEORGE GERSHWIN; 2. LUDWIG VAN BEETHOVEN; 3. GEORGE FRIDERICH HANDEL; 4. PYOTR ILYICH TCHAIKOVSKY 5. RALPH VAUGHAN WILLIAMS; 6. GIACOMO PUCCINI; 7. EDWARD ELGAR; 8. MAURICE RAVEL; 9. FELIX MENDELSSOHN; 10. JOHANN SEBASTIAN BACH.* **MISSING VOWELS ANSWERS:** *1. HOW DO YOU DO? 2. PLEASED TO MEET YOU; 3. WELL PLAYED; 4. CONGRATULATIONS; 5. HARD LUCK.* **TRIVIAtime ANSWER:** *THE WEEKND.*

BACK IN TIME

History time

1. How many of the UK Prime Ministers to serve so far during Queen Elizabeth II's reign, were not born when she came to the throne?

2. Which English king died in 1066, leaving no heir to the throne?

3. Which Hertfordshire town was the first ever New Town after WWII?

4. Which country was the first to give women the right to vote, in 1893?

5. Which famous Queen spent a lot of her childhood at Hertford Castle and Hatfield House?

6. In 1958 the first artificial satellite launched in 1957 fell back to earth. What was its name?

7. Who was the architect that rebuilt London after the Great Fire of 1666?

8. What did the Romans call Scotland?

9. In 1990 who created the World Wide Web?

10. What year was the Potters Bar rail crash which killed 7 people and injured another 76?

GOING STRAIGHT!

3 well-known stars of top UK sit-coms. Can you name them?

BACK IN TIME ANSWERS: *1. 4 (Tony Blair, David Cameron, Theresa May, Boris Johnson) 2. EDWARD THE CONFESSOR; 3. STEVENAGE; 4. NEW ZEALAND; 5. QUEEN ELIZABETH I; 6. SPUTNIK; 7. SIR CHRISTOPHER WREN; 8. CALEDONIA; 9. TIM BERNERS-LEE; 10. 2002.* **GOING STRAIGHT ANSWERS:** *GARY WADHORN, ROGER LLOYD-PACK, ROWAN ATKINSON.*

A NIGHT AT THE OSCARS

And the winners are….

1. How old was Jessica Tandy when she won the Best Actress Oscar for *Driving Miss Daisy* in 1989?

2. *The Godfather* was set in which American city?

3. Who was given the longest standing ovation in Oscar history – 12 minutes – while receiving an Honorary Oscar Award in 1972?

4. Who famously screeched "You like me! Right now, you really like me!" during her Oscar acceptance speech for Best Actress in 1985?

5. Who was the first African American woman to win an Academy Award in the Best Actress category?

6. The first Academy Awards were presented in 1929 at a private dinner, but do you know when they were first televised?   A) 1943   B) 1953   C) 1963

7. Judi Dench and Cate Blanchett, were nominated for playing the same historical figure in 1999 in two different films. Who did they play?

8. What do the films *Ben-Hur*, *Titanic* and *The Lord of the Rings: Return of the King* have in common?

9. The impressive, heavy statue presented at the Academy Awards has been referred to as an 'Oscar' for years, but what is the statue's official name?

10. Which city was Nicholas Cage 'leaving' in his 1995 Oscar-winning performance?

MORPHED IMAGE

Which two TV comedy co-stars make up this morphed image?

A NIGHT AT THE OSCARS ANSWERS: 1. 80; 2. NEW YORK CITY; 3. CHARLIE CHAPLIN; 4. SALLY FIELD; 5. HALLE BERRY (2002 for Monsters Ball); 6. B)1953; 7. ELIZABETH I; 8. THEY EACH WON 11 AWARDS – A RECORD!; 9. THE ACADEMY AWARD OF MERIT; 10. LAS VEGAS. MORPHED IMAGE: VICTORIA WOOD AND JULIE WALTERS.

VICTUALS

Food and Drink to you!

1. Which luxury food shop has been in Piccadilly, London since 1707?

2. How does paella get its name?

3. What is a love apple another name for?

4. With what drink is it considered bad luck to toast someone?

5. What colour is piccalilli?

6. Schnapps is distilled from what?

7. In which country was sherry first produced?

8. What is done to a herring to make it a kipper?

9. How is cook Isabella Mary Mayson better known?

10. In what month does Beaujolais Nouveau arrive?

WHO IS THE SKY DIVER?

Can you identify the international footballer turned TV presenter?

VICTUALS ANSWERS: *1. FORTNUM & MASON; 2. FROM THE PAN IN WHICH IT IS COOKED; 3. TOMATO; 4. WATER; 5. YELLOW; 6. POTATOES; 7. SPAIN; 8. IT IS SMOKED; 9. MRS BEETON; 10. NOVEMBER.* **WHO IS THE SKY DIVER? ANSWER:** *PETER CROUCH*

THIS AND THAT
General knowledge

1. What is the highest peak in Scotland after Ben Nevis?

2. What did Wonder Woman's lasso always make people do?

3. What links Hampstead Heath, Reigate Priory and Maidenhead?

4. Which London Underground line serves Heathrow Airport?

5. Which country has as its anthem, The Soldier's Song?

6. From what did God create Adam?

7. Why did the old lady who swallowed a fly, later swallow a bird?

8. Multiply a soccer team by the cardinal points on a compass, double the figure and divide by 11?

9. Which invention was first applied commercially to a packet of Wrigley's Juicy Fruit chewing gum in 1974?

10. What type of transport was invented by Gottleib Daimler?

MAKE THE CONNECTION 2
4 pictures, what is the connection?

THIS AND THAT ANSWERS: 1. BEN MACDUI; 2. TELL THE TRUTH; 3. ALL WERE ORIGINAL FA CUP ENTRANTS; 4. PICCADILLY LINE; 5. IRELAND; 6. DUST; 7. TO CATCH THE SPIDER; 8. 8; 9. A BAR-CODE; 10. A MOTORCYCLE. MAKE THE CONNECTION 2 ANSWER: GOLDILOCKS AND THE 3 BEARS (BED, BOWLS, PORRIDGE, THREE BEARS (GRYLLS!).

NO. 2 UK HITS OF THE 1970s

10 songs from the 70s that fell just short. Match the songs to the Artistes

1. LET IT BE	A. NEIL REID
2. THE PUSHBIKE SONG	B. OLIVIA NEWTON-JOHN
3. BORN WITH A SMILE ON MY FACE	C. JANET KAY
4. DONNA	D. B.A. ROBERTSON
5. BLACK NIGHT	E. THE BEATLES
6. SILLY GAMES	F. THE MIXTURES
7. HOPELESSLY DEVOTED TO YOU	G. 10cc
8. MOTHER OF MINE	H. SQUEEZE
9. BANG BANG	I. STEPHANIE DE SYKES
10. COOL FOR CATS	J. DEEP PURPLE

FIND THE ELDER!

Four well known faces. Who is the oldest of them?

HOW QUICKLY CAN YOU FIND THE 8?

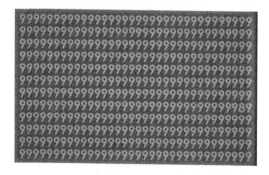

THE MOVIE AIRPLANE! OR DON'T CALL ME SHIRLEY!

How well do you know the film classic from 1980?

1. Which famous composer wrote the music score for *Airplane!*?

2. Ted Striker *(Robert Hays)* meets Elaine *(Julie Hagerty)* in a bar where everyone suddenly breaks into a disco dance. What song is playing?

3. Steve McCrosky *(Lloyd Bridges)* picked the 'wrong week' to quit 4 different things during the film. What were the four things?

4. What former basketball star played the co-pilot?

5. What is the name of the inflatable pilot?

6. What airline is featured in the film?

7. The in-flight meal was fish or steak. What did Dr. Rumack *(Leslie Nielsen)* have for dinner?

8. Ted is haunted by his war time flight over:
A) What target and   B) The trauma left Ted with what problem?

9. In the script. Elaine Dickinson says: A hospital? What is it? What was Dr. Rumack's response?

10. What is odd about the plane's engines?

WRITTEN IN STONE

Can you name the Ten Commandments delivered to Moses?

CITY SILHOUETTES

Can you identify these 10 cities around the world?

MAKE THE CONNECTION 3

4 pictures, what is the connection?

CITY SILHOUETTES ANSWERS: *1. LONDON; 2. NEW YORK; 3. SYDNEY; 4. PARIS; 5. DUBAI; 6. ATHENS; 7. ROME; 8. BRISTOL; 9. DELHI; 10. VANCOUVER.*
MAKE THE CONNECTION 3 ANSWER: *WALLS (Berlin, Hadrian, China, Max).*

VARIED PEOPLE OF INFLUENCE

An assortment of celebrities who have made an impact

1. Which much loved singer known as 'The Forces Sweetheart' died, aged 103 on 18th June 2020?

2. Which former Chancellor of the Exchequer's dance to 'Gangnam Style' on *Strictly Come Dancing* was nominated as a Must-See Moment Award at the 2017 Television BAFTAs?

3. Which rapper was named the most influential Black celebrity in Britain by *The Powerlist* in 2021?

4. What is the name of Billie Elish's acclaimed 2019 debut album?

5. Which singer released her first album *High Expectations* in 2019 and won the Brit Award for Best Female Solo artist in 2020?

6. Which singer has collaborated successfully with Queen and has become active in LGBTQ+ and human rights issues?

7. Which Queen of Rap's attitude got her sacked from 15 jobs before she made it big and now estimated to be worth $85 million?

8. What is the name of *The Chase* chaser who has the nickname The Vixen?

9. Who won the first series of *Ru Paul's Drag Race*?

10. What *Countryfile* and former *One Show* host started his TV career on *Blue Peter*?

VARIED PEOPLE OF INFLUENCE ANSWERS: *1. DAME VERA LYNN; 2. ED BALLS; 3. STORMZY; 4. WHEN WE ALL FALL ASLEEP, WHERE DO WE GO?; 5. MABEL; 6. ADAM LAMBERT; 7.NICKI MINAJ; 8. JENNY RYAN; 9. THE VIVIENNE; 10. MATT BAKER.*

THE VICAR OF DIBLEY –
NO, NO, NO, NO, YES!

Questions about the much-loved sit-com that ran from 1994 to 2007

1. In the first episode, *The Arrival*, what was the name of the vicar who died during a service which just 5 people attended?

2. What is Geraldine's surname?

3. What is the name of the Parish Church of Dibley?

4. What is in Mrs.Cropley's home-made orange juice?

5. Who is the church verger?

6. Which famous singer opens the Dibley Autumn Fayre?

7. Sadly five members of the main cast have now died. Roger Lloyd-Pack (2014), Liz Smith (2016), John Bluthal (2018) and Trevor Peacock (2021) were four of them, but who was the fifth who died in 2018 aged just 53?

8. In the *Animals* episode Hugo takes the Horton family dog to the service as well as Patricia. Who was Patricia?

9. Who were the first people to invite Geraldine for Christmas lunch?

10. Which character said, "I am a great supporter of sex before marriage. Otherwise I wouldn't have had sex at all."

DID YOU KNOW?

TREVOR PEACOCK who plays Jim Trott wrote many hit songs. These include: Gossip Calypso for Bernard Cribbins (No.25 in 1962); Made You for Adam Faith (No. 5 in 1960); Mrs. Brown You've Got a Lovely Daughter for Herman's Hermits (No. 1 in the US in 1965); Mystery Girl for Jess Conrad (No. 18 in 1961) and both Nature's Time For Love a(No. 26 in 1963) and That's What Love Will Do (No. 3 in 1963) for Joe Brown. Other artistes who have recorded his songs include John Barry and Barbra Streisand.

THE VICAR OF DIBLEY OR NO, NO, NO, NO, YES! ANSWERS: *1. REVEREND POTTLE; 2. GRANGER; 3. ST BARNABAS; 4. JUST ORANGE JUICE – SURPRISINGLY!; 5. ALICE TINKER; 6. KYLIE MINOGUE; 7. REVEREND POTTLE; 8. A STUFFED OWL; 9. FRANK PICKLE AND JIM TROTT; 10. OWEN NEWITT.*

REALLY PRIME MINISTER!

Nicknames of some UK Prime Ministers. Match them up!

1. SUPERMAC	A. JAMES CALLAGHAN
2. THE BIG CLUNKING FIST	B. JOHN MAJOR
3. BAMBI	C. THERESA MAY
4. SUNNY JIM	D. CLEMENT ATTLEE
5. THE IRON LADY	E. BORIS JOHNSON
6. GREY MAN	F. HAROLD McMILLAN
7. DORMOUSE AT THE TEA PARTY	G. TONY BLAIR
8. BOJO	H. DAVID LLOYD GEORGE
9. SUBMARINE	J. MARGARET THATCHER
10. WELSH WIZARD	K. GORDON BROWN

MISSING LINK 2

What goes in the fourth box?

FORBIDDEN IN SWIMMING POOLS

There are 9 activities forbidden in public swimming pools. What are they?

MURDER MYSTERY

Hercule Poirot reviewed the information they had on the case so far. A lady named Monica was shot and Poirot had a list of suspects: Kane, Lewandowski, Messi and Ronaldo. The killer is a fan of Poirot and challenges him by leaving notes at various places. # The first was found in the kitchen, # The second was found in an art room. # The third was in the nursery. # the fourth in the entertainment room. All of the notes read the same thing, 'The clues are where you find the notes.' Still, nothing was found anywhere. Poirot paused for a moment and then named the killer. Who was it?

TYING THE KNOT

All about weddings

1. "Ready to face the enemy?" the vicar asks Charles in *Four Weddings and a Funeral*. Who was he about to marry?

2. Which musical includes the song *Get Me to the Church on Time*?

3. Which German composer wrote the piece of music that we now recognise as the *Wedding March*?

4. In which year did Prince Charles marry Camilla Parker-Bowles?

5. Since 1754, over what are weddings traditionally conducted at Gretna Green in Scotland?

6. What is the traditional colour of a bride's dress in China?

7. Who said, "Marriage is a great institution, but I'm not ready for an institution"?

8. Who was best man at David and Victoria Beckham's wedding in 1999?
A) Phil Neville   B) Roy Keane   C) Gary Neville   D) Ryan Giggs

9. *Here Comes the Bride* is part of an 1850 opera, *Lohengrin*. Who composed the opera?

10. Grooms often wear a wide, formal tie. Which sporting event is the accessory named after?

14 WEDDINGS AND A FUNERAL

Listed is music for 14 wedding processions and one funeral procession. Name the odd one out?

1.Canon in D – Pachelbel; 2. Ave Verum Corpus – Mozart; 3. Bridal Chorus – Wagner; 4. Nella Fantasia (or Gabriel's Oboe) - Ennio Morricone; 5. Jesu, Joy of Man Desiring – Bach; 6. The Swan (Le Cygne) - Saint Saens; 7. The Flower Duet from Lakmé (Viens Mallika Sous le Dome) ; 8. Sonata No. 2 in B Flat Minor, 3rd movement – Chopin; 9. Léo Delibes Romance Classical Guitar - folk piece; 10. The Four Seasons: Spring 1 - Vivaldi, Recomposed by Max Richter; 11. Cello suite No. 1 – Bach; 12. Una Furtiva Lagrima - Gaetano Donizetti; 13. A Midsummer Night's Dream Op. 61: IX. 14. Wedding March - Felix Mendelssohn; Ave Maria - Bach/Gounod; 15. Arrival of the Queen of Sheba – Handel.

TYING THE KNOT ANSWERS: *1. HENRIETTA; 2. MY FAIR LADY; 3. FELIX MENDELSSOHN; 4. 2005; 5. BLACKSMITH'S ANVIL; 6. RED; 7. MAE WEST; 8. GARY NEVILLE; 9. RICHARD WAGNER; 10. ASCOT.* **FOURTEEN WEDDINGS AND A FUNERAL ANSWER:** *No 8 is more familiarly known as The Funeral March by Chopin.*

STICK A PONY IN ME POCKET

Only Fools and Horses time!

1. What 3 locations are painted on the Trotters Reliant Regal 3-wheeled van?

2. What was the title of the famous 1982 episode featuring a chandelier?

3. What was the name of the band that featured Rodney and Mental Mickey?

4. How many heads and handles had Trigger's broom had?

5. Who was the only member of the main cast to appear in the prequel series *Rock and Chips*?

6. Who sang the iconic theme song to the show?

7. What nickname does Rodney give to Del's Ford Capri Ghia?

8. What was the name of Del Boy's spring water business?

9. How much did the Harrison Lesser Watch sell for at Sotheby's?

10. In what number Nelson Mandela House do the Trotters live?

MAKE THE CONNECTION 4

Find the link between these 4 pictures

STICK A PONY IN ME POCKET ANSWERS: *1. NEW YORK, PARIS AND PECKHAM; 2. A TOUCH OF GLASS; 3.A BUNCH OF WALLIES; 4. 17 HEADS AND 14 HANDLES; 5. NICHOLAS LYNDHURST; 6. THE WRITE, JOHN SULLIVAN; 7. THE PRATMOBILE; 8. PECKHAM SPRING; 9. £6,200,000; 10. 127.* **MAKE THE CONNECTION 4 ANSWERS:** *PARIS METRO STATIONS: Concorde, George V, Opera, Victor Hugo.*

PROVERBIALLY SPEAKING

Complete these well-known sayings

1. If it ain't broke don't ... it

2. The pen is .... than the sword

3. The ..... makes work for idle hands to do

4. .... starts at home

5. Necessity is the ...... of invention

6. A good man is .... to find

7. No man is an ......

8. A .... rots from the head down

9. Hell hath no fury like a ..... scorned

10. A friend in need is a ...... indeed

GARDENER'S QUESTION TIME

Potting sheds, Allotments, and Backyards

1. Who has presented *Love Your Garden* on ITV since 2011?

2. What garden vegetable is a symbol for Wales?

3. With which county would you associate a White Rose?

4. Who designed the *Blue Peter* Garden in 1974?

5. What colour is the flower speedwell?

6. What is the name for the practice of cutting off spent blooms to encourage new ones?

7. What is the common name for the unwelcome *convolvulus*?

8. True or false. Tulips were once so valuable in Holland that their bulbs were worth more than gold?

9. What fruit comes in varieties Oro Blanco, Ruby Red, Thompson and Pink?

10. *Helianthus* is another name for which flower?

PROVERBIALLY SPEAKING ANSWERS: *1. FIX; 2. MIGHTIER; 3. DEVIL; 4. CHARITY; 5. MOTHER; 6. HARD; 7. ISLAND; 8. FISH; 9. WOMAN; 10. FRIEND.*
GARDENER'S QUESTION TIME ANSWERS: *1. ALAN TITCHMARSH; 2. THE LEEK; 3. YORKSHIRE; 4. PERCY THROWER; 5. BLUE; 6. DEAD HEADING; 7. BINDWEED; 8. TRUE; 9. GRAPEFRUIT; 10. SUNFLOWER.*

TICKLISH ALLSORTS

A general test of your knowledge

1. What is the highest grade of olive oil that can be purchased?

2. Which famous artist had both a 'Rose Period' and a 'Blue Period'?

3. Followers of the Church of Jesus Christ of Latter-day Saints are more commonly known by what single-word name?

4. Paprika is the main spice in which Hungarian meat & vegetable stew?

5. Luzon is the largest and most populous island in which SE Asian nation?

6. What type of clothing is a Glengarry?

7. What is the common name of Ascorbic Acid?

8. What city sinks between 4 to 6" per year because of being built on a lake?

9. What do the following mean in Yuppy Slang?
A) Nimby   B) Woopie   C) Sink

10. Which organisation has the hierarchy positions; Grand Pontiff, Chevalier of the Broken Serpent and Sovereign Grand Inspector General?

CAST OF THE SUMMER WINE

The TV series ran from 1973-2010. Many actors have starred in over 40 episodes. Can you name the 5 stars pictured, and the TV sit-coms that originally made them famous?

TRIVIAtime

'Sweet Caroline' is often heard across the country following England's football successes; but which with Major League Baseball team is the song most associated?

TICKLISH ALLSORTS ANSWERS: *1. EXTRA VIRGIN; 2. PABLO PICASSO; 3. MORMONS; 4. GOULASH; 5. THE PHILIPPINES; 6. A HAT OR BONNET; 7. VITAMIN C; 8. MEXICO CITY; 9. A) NOT IN MY BACKYARD   B) WELL OFF OLDER PERSON   C) SINGLE, INDEPENDENT, NO KIDS; 10. FREEMASONRY.*
CAST OF THE SUMMER WINE ANSWERS: *BRIAN WILDE (Porridge), JUNE WHITFIELD (Terry & June, Absolutely Fabulous etc), FRANK THORNTON (Are You Being Served?), JOSEPHINE TEWSON (Keeping Up Appearances), STEPHEN LEWIS (On the Buses).* **TRIVIAtime ANSWER:** *BOSTON RED SOX.*

YEARS MAY COME ....
What year is outlined in each question?

1. The first Woodstock festival was held. Richard Nixon became president of the USA. The first humans landed on the moon.

2. Elvis Presley died. The Sex Pistols released their only studio album, *Never Mind the Bollocks. Here's the Sex Pistols.* Queen Elizabeth II celebrated her Silver Jubilee.

3. Take That split up. Prince Charles and Princess Diana divorced. The Nintendo 64 was released.

4. The Titanic sunk. The Republic of China was established. The South Pole was discovered.

5. Earl of Rosebery becomes UK Prime Minister. Blackpool Tower opened for the first time.

6. Food rationing in Britain ended when restrictions on the sale and purchase of meat was lifted.

7. A state of emergency in Northern Ireland. 3-day week. Two general elections are held in the UK. Lord Lucan disappeared.

8. Tory party conference was bombed. Mrs. Indira Gandhi assassinated. The first *Terminator* film was shown.

9. John McCarthy taken hostage in Beirut. Space shuttle exploded killing crew of seven. Halley's comet returned. *Today* newspaper was launched.

10. Trial of the Moors murderers. Arkle won the Cheltenham Gold Cup for third year running. The Aberfan disaster. Rhodesia declared a republic.

SONG YEARS
What year is in the title of these hit songs?

1. .... by The Smashing Pumpkins *(Reached No. 16 in 1996)*

2. Disco .... by Pulp *(No. 7 in 1995)*

3. .... by Prince *(No. 2 in 1985, reissued a few times)*

4. December .... (Oh What a Night) by The Four Seasons *(No.1 in 1976)*

5. .... by Estelle *(No. 14 in 2004)*

6. .... by James Blunt *(No. 4 in 2007)*

7. Infinity .... By Guru Josh Project *(No. 3 in 2008)*

8. .... (It Ain't the End) by Jay Sean feat Nicki Minaj *(No. 9 in 2010)*

9. Acapulco .... by Kenny Ball & His Jazzmen *(No. 27 in 1963)*

10. New York Mining Disaster .... by The Bee Gees *(No. 12 in 1967)*

YEARS MAY COME....ANSWERS: *1. 1969; 2. 1977; 3. 1996; 4. 1912; 5. 1894; 6. 1954; 7. 1974; 8. 1984; 9. 1986; 10. 1966.* **SONG YEAR ANSWERS:** *1. 1979; 2. 2000; 3. 1999; 4. 1963; 5. 1980; 6. 1973; 7. 2008; 8. 2012; 9. 1922; 10. 1941.*

THE NAME'S BOND ... JAMES BOND

How well do you know your 007s?

1. What brand of pistol did James Bond prefer, before M forced him to use his Walther in *Dr. No*?

2. How many times has the 'gun barrel scene', that traditionally begins a Bond film, been shot (including all twenty-two films)?

3. The cover name on Bond's business card in *Quantum of Solace* is the same one that Bond gives in which other 007 film?

4. What advertiser's logo was prominent in shots of the aftermath of Jaws' cable car crashing into the cable car station in *Moonraker*?

5. What brand of golf ball, and ball number, did Auric Goldfinger use during his golf match with Bond in *Goldfinger*?

6. Originally known for The Two Ronnies and Eureka on TV, who played Miss Caruso, in the post-opening titles sequence of *Live and Let Die*, the first James Bond film starring Roger Moore?

7. Who is the first character killed in a James Bond movie?

8. What is the name of Madonna's character – a fencing instructor – in *Die Another Day*?

9. Felix Leiter is maimed by a shark in the film Licence to Kill – but in which Ian Fleming novel does this sequence appear?

10. Christopher Lee played Bond villain Scaramanga in *The Man with The Golden Gun* – but what relation was Lee to Bond author Ian Fleming?

BOND FILM SONGS

Match the Bond theme song singers with the bond films?

BOND FILM	THEME SINGER
1. Spectre	A. Carly Simon
2. Casino Royale	B. Chris Cornell
3. From Russia With Love	C. Louis Armstrong
4. For Your Eyes Only	D. Billie Eilish
5. Tomorrow Never Dies	E. Rita Coolidge
6. No Time To Die	F. Sam Smith
7. Skyfall	G. Matt Monro
8. Octopussy	H. Sheryl Crow
9. The Spy Who Loved Me	J. Adele
10. On Her Majesty's Secret Service	K. Sheena Easton

THE NAME'S BOND, JAMES BOND ANSWERS: *1. BARETTA; 2. 9; 3. THE SPY WHO LOVED ME; 4. 7-UP; 5. SLAZENGER 1; 6. MADELINE SMITH; 7. JOHN STRANGWAYS IN DR. NO; 8. VERITY; 9. LIVE AND LET DIE; 10. LEE AND FLEMING WERE COUSINS.* **BOND FILM SONGS ANSWERS:** *1F; 2B; 3G; 4K; 5H, 6D; 7J; 8E; 9A; 10C.*

ONE HIT WONDERS

Can you identify the acts who had just one major hit in their careers?
As a help we list the title of their big hit and the year it hit the charts!

1. 1960
TELL LAURA I LOVE HER

2. 1962
NUT ROCKER

3. 1979
MONEY

4. 1962
BOBBY'S GIRL

5. 1987
PUMP UP THE VOLUME

6. 1978
BRIAN & MICHAEL

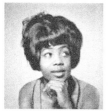

7. 1964
MY BOY LOLLIPOP

8. 2013
SKYSCRAPER

9. 2002
THE KETCHUP SONG

10. 1979
I WILL SURVIVE

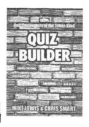
ONE HIT WONDERS ANSWERS: 1. RICKY VALANCE; 2. B BUMBLE & THE STINGERS; 3. FLYING LIZARDS; 4. SUSAN MAUGHAN; 5. M/A/R/R/S; 6. BRIAN & MICHAEL; 7. MILLIE SMALL; 8. SAM BAILEY; 9. LAS KETCHUP; 10. LENA MARTELL.

WE'RE ALL DOOMED!

Questions about the TV sit-com, Dad's Army

1. What is Captain Mainwaring's first name?

2. What was the name of the fictional town where *Dad's Army* was set?

3. Why does Private Pike wear a claret and blue scarf?

4. Which member of the cast was also a successful playwright?

5. Sergeant Wilson had served with distinction during the First World War. what rank did he achieve?

6. Which stamp loving member of the platoon ran the local philately shop but is known more as the local undertaker?

7. Which platoon member would most likely say "Don't panic!"?

8. Who played Chief Warden Hodges?

9. What nickname did Chief Warden William Hodges give to Captain George Mainwaring?

10. Complete this line in the show's famous theme song: "We are the boys who will …."

MAKE THE CONNECTION 5

What connects these four words?

BOWS	ARROWS	SPEAR	CHARIOT

Why was the £50 note featuring scientist Alan Turing being released into circulation on the 23rd June 2021?

WE'RE ALL DOOMED! ANSWERS: 1. GEORGE; 2. WALMINGTON-ON-SEA; 3. IAN LAVENDER IS AN ASTON VILLA FAN; 4. ARNOLD RIDLEY (Godfrey); 5. CAPTAIN; 6. PRIVATE FRAZER; 7. LANCE CORPORAL JACK JONES; 8. BILL PERTWEE; 9. NAPOLEON; 10. 'MAKE YOU THINK AGAIN'. MAKE THE CONNECTION 5 ANSWERS: BLAKE'S LYRICS TO THE HYMN JERUSALEM. TRIVIAtime ANSWER: ANNIVERSARY OF HIS BIRTHDAY (1912).

AROUND BRITAIN

How well do you know our country?

1. Which city do you associate with the following: marmalade, fruit cake, two football teams, jute and *The Beano*?

2. Which fruit was first grown in England at Dorney Court in Buckinghamshire in 1689?

3. What town is known as the second-hand bookshop capital of the world?

4. What house in Norfolk was built by Sir Robert Walpole, Britain's first prime minister, as a second home?

5. The first concentric castle in England was built by Henry II in 1180? Where was it?

6. Britain's only rack-and-pinion railway climbs which mountain?

7. What kind of cheese do they chase down Cooper's Hill?

8. Which king tried to escape by climbing out of a window whilst imprisoned in Carisbrooke Castle, Isle of Wight?

9. What structure stretched 37 miles from modern Bo'ness on the Firth of Forth to Old Kilpatrick on the River Clyde

10. Whose home was Clouds Hill near Wareham, Dorset before he was killed in a motorcycle accident avoiding two boys on their bicycles?

A CAPITAL IDEA

10 countries, 10 capital cities. Match them up.

1. BULGARIA	A. DOHA
2. GRENADA	B. BEIJING
3. PORTUGAL	C. COPENHAGEN
4. SUDAN	D. LUSAKA
5. ZAMBIA	E. VIENNA
6. DENMARK	F. SOFIA
7. QATAR	G. LISBON
8. CHINA	H. SAINT GEORGE'S
9. AUSTRIA	J. KAMPALA
10. UGANDA	K. KHARTOUM

AROUND BRITAIN ANSWERS: *1. DUNDEE; 2. PINEAPPLE; 3. HAY-ON-WYE, BRECONSHIRE; 4. HOUGHTON HALL; 5. DOVER CASTLE; 6. MOUNT SNOWDON; 7. DOUBLE GLOUCESTER; 8. CHARLES I; 9. ANTOINE WALL; 10. T E LAWRENCE (Lawrence of Arabia).* **A CAPITAL IDEA ANSWERS:** *1F, 2H, 3G, 4K, 5D, 6C, 7A, 8B, 9E, 10J.*

KALEIDOSCOPE
A general test

1. Who plays Eve in *Killing Eve*?

2. Who is known as the Money Saving Expert on TV?

3. Who was made Lord Mayor of London in 1397, 1398, 1406 and 1419?

4. Which well known pair live at 62 West Wallaby Street, Wigan, Lancashire?

5. Which fruit contains the highest number of calories?

6. Who was the first African – American female astronaut?

7. On average in Australia how many fatalities each year are caused by venomous snakes?

8. What is the correct term for the unconventional punctuation of a question mark followed by an exclamation mark?

9. How many valves does the heart have?

10. In Harry Potter, what is the name of The Weasley's house?

MAKE THE CONNECTION 6 (x2)
Identify the 8 actresses for 1 point each. Then find a TV connection for all 8.

A   B   C   D

D   E   F   G

KALEIDOSCOPE ANSWERS: *1. SANDRA O; 2. MARTIN LEWIS; 3. RICHARD (DICK) WHITTINGTON; 4. WALLACE & GROMIT; 5. AVOCADO; 6. DR MAE CAROL JEMISON; 7. 2; 8. INTERROBANG; 9. 4 (Mitral, Tricuspid, Aortic, Pulmonic); 10. THE BURROW. .**MAKE THE CONNECTION 6:** TOP ROW. Julie Walters, Patricia Routledge, Eileen Atkins, Stephanie Cole. BOTTOM ROW. Jodie Comer, Maxine Peake, Kristin Scott-Thomas, Harriet Walter. THE CONNECTION IS ALAN BENNETT'S TALKING HEADS. The top 4 were in the originals, the bottom 4 played roles in the 2020 series.*
MAKE THE CONNECTION 6 ANSWERS: *A) DAME JULIE WALTERS; B) PATRICIA ROUTLEDGE; C) EILEEN ATKINS; D) STEPHANIE COLE; E) JODIE COMER; F) MAXINE PEAKE; G) KRISTIN SCOTT-THOMAS G) HARRIET WALTER.*

CONTINUANCE

The answer to each question contains a word repeated in the next answer

1. What does a cooper make for a living?

2. In which Guy Ritchie film did footballer Vinnie Jones make his acting debut in 1998?

3. In which Shakespeare comedy will you find the characters - Valentine, Proteus, Silvia and Julia?

4. In which 1953 musical comedy, based on a 1949 stage musical of the same name, did Marilyn Monroe appear alongside Jane Russell?

5. Which alternative American rock band, who had a 1992 No.2 UK hit with *What's Up*, featured Linda Perry on lead vocals?

6. What is the collective name for the four figures of Christian faith; War, Death, Famine and Pestilence?

7. Colonel Walter E. Kurtz, portrayed by Marlon Brando was the main antagonist of which Francis Ford Coppola movie?

8. Jimmy James and the Vagabonds had 2 hits in the UK in 1976, *I'll Go Where Your Music Takes Me,* and which other song that reached number 5?

9. Which American TV series ran for 30 episodes,1966-1967 starring James Darren & Robert Colbert?

10. What 20km structure connects Italy to Switzerland through the Alps?

MISSING LINK 5

What should appear in the fourth box to complete the acronym?

NOVEMBER	ALPHA	TANGO	?

CONTINUANCE ANSWERS: *1. BARRELS; 2. LOCK, STOCK AND TWO SMOKING BARRELS; 3. TWO GENTLEMEN OF VERONA; 4. GENTLEMEN PREFER BLONDES; 5. FOUR NON BLONDES; 6. FOUR HORSEMEN OF THE APOCALYPSE; 7. APOCALYPSE NOW; 8. NOW IS THE HOUR; 9. THE TIME TUNNEL; 10. THE SIMPLON TUNNEL.* **MISSING LINK 5:** *OSCAR (Initials of the NATO alphabet used in communications).*

BITS AND PIECES
All sorts of stuff

1. What are Altostratus, Cumulonimbus and Stratus?

2. Red sky at night, shepherd's delight; red sky in the morning shepherd's …….. Complete the proverb!

3. What connects Tor, Gawain and Lancelot?

4. Which woman won the Nobel Prize for Physics in 1903, and also for Chemistry in 1911?

5. What game uses the following terms: Stalemate, Skewer and Bad Bishop?

6. What links Paul McCartney, Elizabeth II and Phil Collins?

7. What is the national animal of Scotland?

8. What's longer, a nautical mile or a mile?

9. What is someone who believes in antidisestablishmentarianism opposed to the disestablishment of?

10. Who has been the longest serving presenter of the BBC children's television show *Blue Peter*?

EVENTS OF THE DECATHLON

**The decathlon comprises 10 track and field events.
For one point each, can you name them in the order they are competed by the men?**

*On your marks!
Event number one to get you started.*

BITS AND PIECES ANSWERS: *1. TYPES OF CLOUD; 2. WARNING; 3. KNIGHTS OF THE ROUND TABLE; 4. MARIE CURIE; 5. CHESS; 6. ALL LEFT-HANDED; 7. UNICORN; 8. NAUTICAL MILE (1.15 miles); 9. THE CHURCH OF ENGLAND; 10. JOHN NOAKES (12 years 1965-78).* **EVENTS OF THE DECATHLON ANSWERS:** *100 METRES, LONG JUMP, SHOT PUTT, HIGH JUMP, 400 METRES, 110 METRES HURDLES, DISCUS, POLE VAULT, JAVELIN, 1500 METRES.*

MURDER MOST FOUL

A round about awful, unlawful acts

1. Ethel Le Neve was which murderer's typist and mistress?

2. Who was widely assumed to have been responsible for ordering the 1929 Saint Valentine's Day Massacre of seven men?

3. In what district of London did Jack the Ripper prey on women in 1888?

4. Christopher Craig shot a Policeman in 1952, but who hung for the crime?

5. How old was the Yorkshire Ripper when he was finally fortuitously captured after a five-year killing spree?

6. PC Keith Blakelock was killed during which riots in London in 1985?

7. Norman Lewis's 1974 novel *The Sicilian Specialist* is allegedly based upon the assassination plot to kill whom?

8. Peter Hogg killed his wife and dumped her body in a lake in 1976. 8 years later The Lady in the Lake's body was discovered. In which lake?

9. John Reginald Halliday Christie was a serial killer and necrophile from Halifax, active in the 1940s and early 1950s. He strangled at least eight people, including his wife, Ethel in his flat at which address?

10. Writer Joe Orton was bludgeoned to death by his partner, with nine hammer blows to the head, at their home in Islington, London. His partner then killed himself. What was his name?

SIX SOCCER SNIPPETS!

All refer to the men's game of football and facts as at October 2021

1. Which two European players have won the most international caps?

2. Who is the only player to have won more than 100 caps for Wales?

3. Who is the most capped footballer from one of the home nations?

4. Which England outfielder won the most caps without ever scoring a goal?
A) Gary Neville   B) Bobby Moore   C) Ashley Cole   D) Sol Campbell

5. Which forward scored more international goals than he won caps?

6. Which Premier League manager won an international cap as a player?
A) Mikel Arteta   B) Steve Bruce   C) Ralph Hasenhüttl   D) Claudio Ranieri

MURDER MOST FOUL ANSWERS: *1. DR. HAWLEY HARVEY CRIPPEN; 2. AL CAPONE; 3. WHITECHAPEL; 4. DEREK BENTLEY; 5. 34 YEARS OLD; 6. BROADWATER FARM, TOTTENHAM; 7. JOHN F KENNEDY; 8. WAST WATER, WASDALE IN THE LAKE DISTRICT; 9. 10 RILLINGTON PLACE, NOTTING HILL, LONDON; 10. KENNETH HALLIWELL.* **SIX SOCCER SNIPPETS ANSWERS:** *1. SERGIO RAMOS & CHRISTIANO RONALDO (180); 2. CHRIS GUNTER (104); 3. STEVEN DAVIS (128 FOR NORTHERN IRELAND); 4. ASHLEY COLE (104); 5. GERD MÜLLER (68 GOALS IN 62 MATCHES); 6. C) RALPH HASENHÜTTL (8 AUSTRIA CAPS)*

CORRELATION

Answer the 10 questions and find the connection

1. Which J.M. Barrie character, in a famous children's story, was stalked by a ticking crocodile?

2. What was the name of the roan Cocker Spaniel, with long black ears, who joined *The Sooty Show* in 1957?

3. What is the name of a closely cropped hairstyle, so named because it was originally worn by teams of rowers?

4. What is a web browser developed by Microsoft. It was first released for Windows 10 and X-box One in 2015?

5. What was the title of the song by *The Cars* that reached No. 5 in the UK in 1984 (No. 4 on re-entry in 1985) to become their second highest chart entry after *There She Goes*?

6. What type of bird is a velvet scoter?

7. What is the name for a person employed by a nightclub or similar venue to prevent troublemakers and other unwanted people entering or to eject them from the premises?

8. By what name is the expert marksman and fighter, Clint Barton who works for S.H.I.E.L.D. as a special agent, known?

9. What was the name of the sit-com series based around the activities and problems of running the local cricket team, starring Robert Daws, Brenda Blethyn, Timothy Spall and Josie Lawrence?

10. What is a short pole with a wide, flat part at one end or both ends, used for moving a small boat or canoe through the water called?

CHURCHILL CLONES

Many actors have portrayed Winston Churchill. Here are 5 of them to identify.

CORRELATION ANSWERS: 1. CAPTAIN HOOK; 2. SWEEP; 3. A CREW CUT; 4. MICROSOFT EDGE; 5. DRIVE; 6. A SEA DUCK; 7. A BOUNCER; 8. HAWKEYE; 9. OUTSIDE EDGE; 10. PADDLE (scoop or pull. THE CONNECTION IS THE GAME OF CRICKET. CHURCHILL CLONES ANSWERS: A) GARY OLDMAN, B) IAN McNEICE, C) BRIAN COX, D) ALBERT FINNEY, E) TIMOTHY SPALL.

WE SHALL NEVER SURRENDER

Questions about Sir Winston Churchill

1. In which category did Winston Churchill win a Nobel Prize?

2. In which palace was Churchill born?

3. In 1899, Churchill lost a by-election in Oldham representing which party?

4. In the famous wartime speech Churchill said, 'I have nothing to offer but ....' What four things?

5. Which sport did Churchill enjoy whilst a young man?
A) Football   B) Polo   C) Golf   D) Rugby

6. In 2002 the BBC held a 100 Greatest Britons poll. Who were the top 3?

7. What was the breed of Churchill's dog Rufus?

8. When Churchill said, "Never in the field of human conflict was so much owed by so many to so few", who did he mean by "so few"?

9. In what war was Churchill taken prisoner and then escaped?

10. What was the name of the country estate purchased by Churchill?

CHRISTMAS UK NUMBER ONES

Who had the top single with these songs in these years?

1. IT'S ONLY MAKE BELIEVE (1958)

2. MOON RIVER (1961)

3. LONG HAIRED LOVER FROM LIVERPOOL (1972)

4. ONLY YOU (1983)

5. ALWAYS ON MY MIND (1987)

6. SOMETHIN' STUPID (2001)

7. A MOMENT LIKE THIS (2006)

8. HE AIN'T HEAVY, HE'S MY BROTHER (2012)

9. SOMETHING I NEED (2014)

10. I LOVE SAUSAGE ROLLS (2019)

WE SHALL NEVER SURRENDER ANSWERS: *1. LITERATURE; 2. BLENHEIM PALACE; 3. CONSERVATIVE; 4. BLOOD, TOIL, TEARS, SWEAT; 5. B) POLO; 6. 1. SIR WINSTON CHURCHILL; 2. ISAMBARD KINGDOM BRUNEL; 3. DIANA, PRINCESS OF WALES; 7. POODLE; 8. AIRMEN DEFENDING THE UK IN THE BATTLE OF BRITAIN; 9. THE SECOND BOER WAR; 10. CHARTWELL.*
CHRISTMAS UK NUMBER ONES ANSWERS: *1. CONWAY TWITTY; 2. DANNY WILLIAMS; 3. LITTLE JIMMY OSMOND; 4. FLYING PICKETS; 5. PET SHOP BOYS; 6. ROBBIE WILLIAMS & NICOLE KIDMAN; 7. LEONA LEWIS; 8. THE JUSTICE COLLECTIVE; 9. BEN HAENOW; 10. LADBABY.*

NAME & FAME

Identify these 11 men and find the sporting achievement that links them

LAST LETTER, FIRST LETTER
The last letter of answer1 will be the first letter of answer 2 and so on

1. What is the regional capital of Campania and the third-largest city of Italy after Rome and Milan, with a population of almost a million?

2. Name the prison that holds Norman Stanley Fletcher.

3. Name the country straddling the equator on South America's west coast with a diverse landscape covering Amazon jungle, Andean highlands and the wildlife-rich Galápagos Islands.

4. What is the full name of the leading composer of the late Romantic and Early Modern eras, whose best-known composition is probably the tone poem *Also Sprach Zarathustra*?

5. What is the name of the actress who was born on 20 September 1934 in Rome who has starred in many films including A Countess From Hong Kong, Two Women, The Millionairess and many more and also had a hit record, *Goodness Gracious Me*, with Peter Sellers?

6. What chemical compound is commonly known as laughing gas? At room temperature, it is a colourless non-flammable gas, with a slight metallic scent and taste.

7. Which cultural icon of the 20th century notched up 21 number one hits and whose first hit was in 1955 with I'm Left, You're Right, She's Gone?

8. What is the resort city on the south coast of the Crimean Peninsula surrounded by the Black Sea that hosted a famous conference in 1945?

9. What is the last name of the monomaniacal fictional captain of the whaling ship Pequod who lost a leg to the whale Moby Dick, and who had a prosthetic leg made from whalebone?

10. Who is the Scottish singer and actress whose solo hits include *Answer Me* and *January, February* and also a massive No. 1 with Elaine Paige and who has released over 30 albums since 1970?

LAST LETTER, FIRST LETTER ANSWERS: 1. NAPLES; 2. SLADE; 3. ECUADOR; 4. RICHARD STRAUSS; 5. SOPHIA LOREN; 6. NITROUS OXIDE; 7. ELVIS PRESLEY; 8. YALTA; 9. AHAB; 10. BARBARA DICKSON.

A-B-C-D
Multi-choice round

1. What garden features were banned from the Chelsea Flower Show until 2013?   A) Bird baths   B) Gazebos   C) Gnomes   D) Decking

2. Which Stephen King novel features the character Jack Torrance?
A) Carrie   B) Salem's Lot   C) The Shining   D) The Green Mile

3. Which legendary character has been portrayed by both Sir Sean Connery and his son Jason?   A) King Arthur   B) Galahad   C) Merlin   D) Robin Hood

4. If 'Thorpe' is present in a place name, it indicates the settlement started as a Viking what?   A) Farm   B) Forge   C) Fort   D) Filling station

5. What is the colour of Donald Duck's bow tie?
A) Red   B) Yellow   C) Blue   D) White

6. What company published the Mario Kart video game?
A) Nintendo   B) Sega   C) EA   D) Microsoft

7. In Ray Bradbury's novel *Fahrenheit 451* what is being burnt?
A) Clothes   B) Houses   C) Books   D) Money

8. In 2016 a musician won the Nobel Peace prize for Literature. Who was it?
A) Lenny Kravitz   B) Eric Clapton   C) Elton John   D) Bob Dylan

9. How many feet in a mile?   A) 1037   B) 5288   C) 5280   D) 6201

10. In 1945 what caused a 5-minute delay to Big Ben?   A) Lunar eclipse
B) A German bomb   C) Starlings landing on minute hand   D) Lightning

How many sunflowers were there in Van Gogh's third version of the painting 'Sunflowers'?

A-B-C-D ANSWERS: *1. C) GNOMES; 2. C) THE SHINING; 3. D)ROBIN HOOD; 4. A) FARM; 5. A) RED; 6. A) NINTENDO; 7. C) BOOKS; 8. D) BOB DYLAN; 9. C) 5280; 10. C) STARLINGS LANDING ON MINUTE HAND.* **TRIVIAtime ANSWER:** *12.*

WHAT A BUNCH OF CHARLIES

Various Questions about men called Charles

1. Name the English inventor of a calculating machine that was the forerunner of the computer.

2. Who was the great English novelist of the Victorian era who created some of the world's best-known fictional characters including Oliver Twist?

3. Which French army officer and statesman famously said 'Non' to Britain joining the European Union?

4. Who became Duke of Cornwall in 1952?

5. Which English comic and film star was banned from re-entering the US in 1952 for being 'un-American'?

6. Bonnie Prince Charlie escaped to Skye dressed as 'Betty Burke', leading to his portrayal as a romantic figure of heroic failure, after what 1746 battle?

7. Who was the English musician who achieved international fame as the drummer of the Rolling Stones from 1963 until his death in August 2021?

8. Name the show promoter and businessman who founded the famous annual London Dog Show, who died aged 86 in 1938?

9. Who was the legendary French tightrope walker and acrobat who made several crossings of Niagara Falls, initially in 1859?

10. Identify the American actor who, until 1954 used his real name, Charles Buchinsky, before starring in many films including the *Death Wish* series?

DENZEL WASHINGTON MOVIES

10 movies, 10 characters. Match them up.

1. THE MAGNIFICENT SEVEN	A. ROBERT McCALL
2. TRAINING DAY	B. LINCOLN RHYME
3. PHILADELPHIA	C. ALONZO
4. DÉJÀ VU	D. DOUG CARLIN
5. THE EQUALIZER	E. TOBIN FROST
6. THE BONE COLLECTOR	F. CHISOLM
7. 2 GUNS	G. FRANK LUCAS
8. SAFE HOUSE	H. JOE MILLER
9. AMERICAN GANGSTER	J. WALTER GARBER
10. TAKING OF PELHAM 1-2-3	K. BOBBY

WHAT A BUNCH OF CHARLIES ANSWERS: *1. CHARLES BABBAGE; 2. CHARLES DICKENS; 3. CHARLES DE GAULLE; 4. PRINCE CHARLES; 5. CHARLIE CHAPLIN; 6. CULLODEN; 7. CHARLIE WATTS; 8. CHARLES CRUFT; 9. CHARLES BLONDIN; 10. CHARLES BRONSON.* **DENZEL WASHINGTON MOVIES ANSWERS:** *1F, 2C, 3H, 4D, 5A, 6B, 7K, 8E, 9G, 10J.*

LUCKY SEVEN
All about the number 7

1. Kevin Keegan netted 100 goals for Liverpool. Which other legendary number 7 succeeded him to become arguably the club's greatest ever player?

2. Morgan Freeman and Brad Pitt chased serial killer Kevin Spacey in the 1995 thriller *Se7en*. Who played Pitt's unhappy wife Tracy?

3. Who wrote the autobiographical account *The Seven Pillar of Wisdom* ?

4. What is the lemon-lime-flavored non-caffeinated soft drink manufactured by Keurig Dr. Pepper?

5. In the song *The 12 Days of Christmas*, what was the gift on the 7th day?

6. In the novel *The Seven Per Cent Solution* by Nicholas Meyer, filmed in 1976; which famous private detective, travels to Vienna to seek psychiatric help from Sigmund Freud?

7. Name the Brothers Grimm story made into a 1937 animated musical fantasy film produced by Walt Disney Productions?

8. What is a nickname given to surgeons who tend to kill their patients, originating from James Bond's code number, which means "License to kill."?

9. A) Who played the leader of The Magnificent Seven in the original film in 1960 and B) who wrote the famous music score?

10. In which 1955 film did Marilyn Monroe's skirt get blown upwards by air from a grating?

MAKE THE CONNECTION 7
4 pictures, can you find a link?

LUCKY SEVEN ANSWERS: *1. KENNY DALGLISH; 2. GWYNETH PALTROW; 3. T E LAWRENCE (Lawrence of Arabia); 4. 7-UP; 5. SEVEN-SWANS-A-SWIMMING; 6. SHERLOCK HOLMES; 7. SNOW WHITE AND THE SEVEN DWARFS; 8. 007; 9. A) YUL BRYNNER, B) ELMER BERNSTEIN; 10. THE SEVEN YEAR ITCH.*
MAKE THE CONNECTION 6: *IF THEY ARE UPSIDE DOWN THEY REPRESENT BAD LUCK OR NEGATIVITY. Horseshoe is unlucky, Union Jack is a sign of distress, Justice tarot card indicates unfairness, Thumbs down registers disapproval.*

SELECTION BOX

A mixed bag of questions

1. Big Willy and Little Willy were the first types of what kind of war machine?

2. What sort of beans are a main ingredient of chilli con carne?

3. Which Australian outlaw did Mick Jagger portray in a 1970 film?

4. What is the literal meaning of the Italian 'Tiramisu' pudding?

5. What eye condition is also the name of a type of waterfall?

6. What was a brass monkey?

7. For what crime was Anne Boleyn executed in 1536?

8. 'Galvayne's Groove' can be used to determine the age of what?

9. If you had a 'Cambridge Rival' in your mouth, what would you be eating?

10. What is made from a mixture of linseed oil and powdered chalk?

WHAT AM I?

5 clues to find out. The quicker you get the answer, the more points you get

5 POINTS. This mystery animal feeds on grass and herbs and is a protected species. Decreasing numbers due to them being hunted for their skins and being used for food.

4 POINTS. Found primarily on the savannah of Africa. Several species including Grevy's and Plains.

3 POINTS. The quagga, declared extinct in the 19th century, was a sub-species of this animal.

2 POINTS. The female gives birth after a gestation of 13 months. Young can run within 14 minutes.

1 POINT. This equine creature is noted for its black and white striped coat.

SELECTION BOX ANSWERS: *1. TANKS; 2. KIDNEY BEANS; 3. NED KELLY; 4. PICK ME UP; 5. CATARACT; 6. BRASS RACK TO HOLD CANNONBALLS. IN COLD WEATHER IT WOULD EJECT THE BALLS*; 7. ADULTERY; 8. A HORSE; 9. A STRAWBERRY; 10. PUTTY.* * Hence the expression to freeze the balls off a brass monkey. ***QUIZ 80 – WHAT AM I? ANSWER: ZEBRA.***

MORE THIS AND THAT

Diversity of knowledge

1. What was the nickname of the woman who is commemorated by the Crimean Monument in Waterloo Place, London?

2. Who was the alter ego — Dr Jekyll or Mr Hyde?

3. Edward I, the father of 18 legitimate children, was called 'Longshanks' because of the length of his what?

4. Aspirin was first synthesised from the bark of which riverbank tree?

5. The passengers of the Titanic waved goodbye to which British port?

6. In 2019, London was the UK's most popular tourist destination. Which City was the second most popular?

7. Who was the heaviest. Sylvester Stallone as Rocky; former Labour politician John Prescott or Elvis Presley at the time of his death?

8. Which is the oldest of these chocolate bars: Fry's Turkish Delight; Cadbury's Dairy Milk or Fry's Chocolate Cream?

9. Which famous statesman was born in a ladies' room during a dance?

10. Which murderer, convicted in 1995 for the murder of 9 women, was given a whole life tariff, only the second time a woman has received that sentence in the UK in modern times?

STARRY, STARRY NIGHT

How much, or little, do you know about the troubled Dutch painter Vincent van Gogh?

1. How many paintings did Van Gogh sell during his lifetime?

2. Where will you find the Vincent Van Gogh Museum?

3. Which of his ears did Van Gogh cut off?

4. Which painting by Van Gogh sold for £22.5m at a Christie's, London auction in 1987?

5. How did Van Gogh kill himself?

AT THE MOVIES
Film Trivia Round

1. *The Imitation Game* is a biopic based on which twentieth century figure?

2. Which actor got his big break playing a lonely schoolboy in *About A Boy*?

3. Meryl Streep won a Best Actress BAFTA for which 2011 political drama?

4. Name the two actresses who portrayed Vesper Lynd in *Casino Royale* in the 1967 and 2006 versions.

5. What is the name of Humphrey Bogart's character in *Casablanca*?

6. Who has won the most Oscars for acting in the history of the Academy Awards?

7. What are the names of the twins played by Lindsay Lohan in the 1998 remake of *The Parent Trap*?

8. What is the first word spoken in *Star Wars: The Empire Strikes Back*?

9. Which Shakespearean actor directed the first *Thor* movie?

10. Who starred as astronaut Neil Armstrong in Damien Chazelle's biopic *First Man*?

TEST MATCH STATUS
12 ranked countries play Test Cricket. Can you name them?

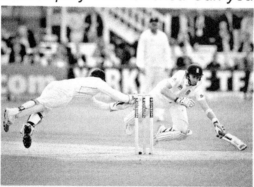

AT THE MOVIES ANSWERS: *1. ALAN TURING; 2. NICHOLAS HOULT; 3. THE IRON LADY; 4. URSULA ANDRESS AND EVA GREEN; 5. RICK BLAINE; 6. KATHERINE HEPBURN, 7. HALLIE AND ANNIE; 8. ECHO; 9. SIR KENNETH BRANAGH; 10. RYAN GOSLING.* **TEST MATCH STATUS ANSWERS:** *As at October 2021. AFGHANISTAN, AUSTRALIA, BANGLADESH, ENGLAND, INDIA, IRELAND, NEW ZEALAND, PAKISTAN, SOUTH AFRICA, SRI LANKA, WEST INDIES, ZIMBABWE.*

A MATTER OF READING
A novel idea for a round

1. Which English author wrote her only novel, *Black Beauty*, in the last years of her life when she was an invalid, dying just 5 months after its publication?

2. Which dystopian novel features the characters Julia, O'Brien and Emmanuel Goldstein? Who wrote the book?

3. Which author wrote the *Foundation* series of science fiction novels?

4. Which prolific crime writer includes *The Big Four, Peril at End House* and *Curtain* in their bibliography of 66 detective and mystery novels?

5. A Michael Crichton novel was turned into a 1993 screen blockbuster by Steven Spielberg. What was the title?

6. Ian Fleming is famous for writing the James Bond novels. However, he also wrote a story that became which 1968 hit musical film?

7. What is the first part of J.R.R. Tolkien's *Lord of the Rings* trilogy called?

8. J, George and Harris form the eponymous title of which book by Jerome K. Jerome where they go on a boating holiday with Montmorency the dog?

9. Who wrote the classic adventure story about Phileas Fogg and his newly employed French valet's attempt to circumnavigate the world?

10. Who is the main character in John Buchan's *The Thirty-Nine-Steps*?

U.K. NATIONAL PARKS
There are 15 National Parks in the UK. Can you name them?

A MATTER OF READING ANSWERS: 1. ANNA SEWELL; 2. A) 1984, B) GEORGE ORWELL; 3.ISAAC ASIMOV; 4. DAME AGATHA CHRISTIE; 5. JURASSIC PARK; 6. CHITTY CHITTY BANG BANG; 7. THE FELLOWSHIP OF THE RING; 8. THREE MEN IN A BOAT; 9. JULES VERNE (Around the World in 80 Days); 10. RICHARD HANNAY. **U.K. NATIONAL PARKS ANSWERS:** ENGLAND - Broads, Dartmoor, Exmoor, Lake District, New Forest, Northumberland, North York Moors, Peak District, Yorkshire Dales and South Downs. WALES - Brecon Beacons, Pembrokeshire Coast, and Snowdonia. SCOTLAND - Cairngorms and Loch Lomond & the Trossachs.

COMMON SENSE
General Knowledge stuff

1. Who scored England's only try in the 2003 Rugby World Cup Final win?

2. What is the only anagram of the word MONDAY?

3. What is the only fruit to have seeds on the outside?

4. Telephone numbers beginning '01418' are most commonly associated with which Scottish city?

5. Where did the Muffin Man live?

6. What did Edward Love invent: power steering, cat litter or air conditioning?

7. In the game Cluedo, which room can be accessed via the secret passage from the study?

8. In which year was DNA discovered? A) 1947   B) 1953   C) 1967   D) 1983

9. On which day of the week was the 9/11 attack on the World Trade Centre?

10. Which billionaire businessman began his career selling plastic ducks from a small apartment?

THE CURSE OF DRACULA
5 biting questions about the Count

1. Who created the literary character of Count Dracula?

2. Transylvania, the home of Dracula, is a central region in which country?

3. In the novel, in which seaside town does Dracula come ashore from the ship Demeter?

4. Which member of the onion family is repellent to vampires?

5. For which British film company did Christopher Lee make numerous appearances as Dracula?

COMMON SENSE ANSWERS: *1. JASON ROBINSON; 2. DYNAMO; 3. STRAWBERRY; 4. GLASGOW; 5. ON DRURY LANE; 6. CAT LITTER; 7. THE KITCHEN; 8. B) 1953; 9. TUESDAY; 10. ROMAN ABRAMOVITCH.*
THE CURSE OF DRACULA ANSWERS: *1. BRAM STOKER; 2. ROMANIA; 3. WHITBY; 4. GARLIC; 5. HAMMER.*

THE UK AND THE EUROVISION SONG CONTEST

Like it or hate it! NAME THE ACTS AND HOW THEY DID!

1. 1961
2. 1965
3. 1967
4. 1969
5. 1975
6. 1976
7. 1981
8. 1989
9. 1997
10. 1998

FOOTBALL FABLES

True or False?

1. The phrase 'park the bus' arose when Jose Mourinho was forced to park the Chelsea team bus after the bus driver fell ill.

2. Former Brazil and Barcelona star Ronaldinho spent time in prison after being found to have used a fake passport.

3. It took Cristiano Ronaldo 1070 minutes to score his first Champions League goal.

THE U.K. AND THE EUROVISION SONG CONTEST ANSWERS: *All these acts finished 1ST or 2nd for the UK. The last time we won was 1997. 1. THE ALLISONS (Are You Sure 2nd; 2. KATHY KIRBY (I Belong 2nd); 3. SANDIE SHAW (Puppet on a String 1st); 4. LULU (Boom Bang-a-Bang = 1st); 5. THE SHADOWS (Let Me Be the One 2nd); 6. BROTHERHOOD OF MAN (Save Your Kisses For Me 1st); 7. BUCKS FIZZ (Making Your Mind Up 1st); 8. LIVE REPORT (Why Do I Always Get It Wrong? 2nd); 9. KATRINA & WAVES (Shine A Light On Me 1st); 10. IMAANI (Where Are You 2nd).*
FOOTBALL FABLES ANSWERS: *1. FALSE; 2. TRUE; 3; TRUE.*

CONTINUITY QUIZ

Each answer contains a word that is repeated in the answer to the next question

1. In which TV sit-com did Will Smith play a rapper who left Philadelphia to live with wealthy relatives?

2. Who did Flora McDonald help to escape to the Isle of Skye?

3. Who appeared as himself singing the song *Behind Closed Doors* in the Clint Eastwood film *Every Which Way But Loose*?

4. Which novel by Irwin Shaw told the story of the Jordache family?

5. In which film is the main villain named Scaramanga?

6. The building of what structure was completed in San Francisco in May 1937?

7. Which film recounted the true story of the 1944 Battle of Arnhelm?

8. Bathsheba Everdene is the heroine of which Thomas Hardy novel?

9. What was The Beatles first number one single in the UK in 1963?

10. In which 2000 film did Jim Carrey play a character suffering from Schizophrenia?

THE ADVENTURES OF BASIL FAWLTY

Four stills from Fawlty Towers. Name the episodes.

CONTINUITY QUIZ ANSWERS: 1. THE PRINCE OF BELAIR; 2. BONNIE PRINCE CHARLIE; 3. CHARLIE RICH; 4. RICH MAN, POOR MAN; 5. THE MAN WITH THE GOLDEN GUN; 6. THE GOLDEN GATE BRIDGE; 7. A BRIDGE TOO FAR; 8. FAR FROM THE MADDING CROWD; 9. FROM ME TO YOU; 10. ME, MYSELF AND IRENE. **THE ADVENTURES OF BASIL FAWLTY ANSWERS:** A. GOURMET NIGHT; B. THE HOTEL INSPECTORS; C. COMMUNICATION PROBLEMS; D. WALDORF SALAD.

WHAT DO YOU EXPECT TO SEE OUT OF A TORQUAY HOTEL WINDOW?

A round about TV sit-com Fawlty Towers

1. Who co-wrote the show with John Cleese?

2. Which two chefs are seen in the kitchen at *Fawlty Towers*?

3. Where does Basil end up at the end of *The Kipper and the Corpse* episode?

4. When the Germans arrive what does Basil say it is important not to mention?

5. Basil thinks that Mr. Hutchinson is a hotel inspector. What is his actual job?

6. What does Sybil use to hit O'Reilly in *The Builders*?

7. What hobby does Polly have in her spare time?

8. From what city is Manuel?

9. What is the number, street and town of the *Fawlty Towers* address?

10. Lord Melbury intends to con Basil out of his collection of:
A) Stamps   B) Cigarette cards   C) Coins   D) Victorian postcards

Two Tests For Your Brain

A lift is on the ground floor. There are four people in the lift including me. When the lift reaches first, floor, one person gets out and three people get in. The lift goes up to the second floor, 2 people get out 6 people get in. It then goes up to the next floor up, no-one gets out, but 12 people get in. Halfway up to the next floor up the lift cable snaps, it crashes to the floor. Everyone else dies in the lift. How did I survive?

ANSWER: I exited the lift on the second floor

I left my campsite and hiked south for 3 miles. Then I turned east and hiked for 3 miles. I then turned north and hiked for 3 miles; at which time I came upon a bear inside my tent eating my food! What colour was the bear?

ANSWER: White. The only place you can hike 3 miles south, then east for 3 miles, then north for 3 miles and up back at your starting point is the North Pole. There are only polar bears in the North Pole, and they are white!

THE YEAR 2012
It all happened in that year

1. Troops had to step in after which security company failed to provide enough temporary staff for the London Olympics?

2. What was the name of the cruise ship that ran aground off Tuscany?

3. What rose from 46p to 60p in April 2012?

4. Which electrical retail chain, bought by Opcapita for the nominal sum of £2 in 2011, had to call in the administrators?

5. Which American jumped from a balloon 24 miles above earth to become the first skydiver to reach the speed of sound?

6. After 244 years since first being published, what source of joy and learning discontinued its print edition?

7. Which Irish singer made UK chart history by becoming the first artist to have an album in the UK charts each year for 25 years consecutively?

8. What is Albert, a stuffed creature upon which the Foreign Office spent £10,000 for essential maintenance?

9. What name was given to the Hurricane that devastated portions of the Caribbean, mid-Atlantic and North East USA?

10. Which famous steam engine celebrated 150 years in operation?

LYRICS
Lyrics to 5 songs. Can you name the artistes and songs?

1. "Took four long years to call it quits, forget that boy, I'm over it."
2. "Now the day bleeds into nightfall, and you're not here to get me through it all."
3. "I wanna hold 'em like they do in Texas, please."
4. "Come on now, follow my lead, I may be crazy, don't mind me."
5. "All my girls 'round the world, I know you know what I mean."

THE YEAR 2012 ANSWERS: *1. G4S; 2. COSTA CONCORDIA; 3. FIRST CLASS POSTAGE STAMPS; 4. COMET; 5. FELIX BAUMGARTNER; 6. ENCYCLOPAEDIA BRITANNICA; 7. DANIEL O'DONNELL; 8. AN ANACONDA (Suspended from the ceiling of the library); 9. SANDY; 10. THE FLYING SCOTSMAN.*
LYRICS ANSWERS: *1. LITTLE MIX – SHOUT OUT TO MY EX; 2. LEWIS CAPALDI – SOMEONE YOU LOVED; 3. LADY GAGA – POKER FACE; 4. ED SHEERAN – SHAPE OF YOU; 5. MABEL – BOYFRIEND.*

MOVIE CLOSING LINES

Name the movies that ended with the following lines:

1. "Hang on lads; I've got a great idea."

2. "I do wish we could chat longer, but I'm having an old friend for dinner."

3. "Louis, I think this is the beginning of a beautiful friendship."

4. "Oh, no! It wasn't the airplanes. It was beauty killed the beast."

5. "Well, nobody's perfect."

6. "I was cured all right."

7. "It's a strange world, isn't it?"

8. "Roads? Where we're going, we don't need roads."

9. "It was perfect."

10. "This is Ripley, last survivor of the Nostromo, signing off."

ROBIN AND THE MERRY MEN

Take from the rich and give to the poor

1. What kind of animal did Disney use to portray Robin Hood in their animated version of the story?

2. Which right-hand man of Robin Hood is renowned for his size & strength?

3. When Kevin Costner played Robin Hood on film, who played Maid Marian?

4. What is the name of the principal sworn enemy of Robin Hood, played most memorably by Alan Rickman?

5. In which English county is Sherwood Forest, the hideout of Robin Hood?

6. Which man of the cloth did Robin reputedly fight at Fountain Dale before inviting him to join the band?

7. What is the name of Robin Hood's minstrel?

8. Who was known as Robin Hood of Texas?

9. Who played Robin in the 1950s TV series *The Adventures of Robin Hood*?

10. Who played the title role in the 1938 film The Adventures of Robin Hood?

MOVIE CLOSING LINES ANSWERS: *1. THE ITALIAN JOB; 2. SILENCE OF THE LAMBS; 3. CASABLANCA; 4. KING KONG; 5. SOME LIKE IT HOT; 6. A CLOCKWORK ORANGE; 7. BLUE VELVET; 8. BACK TO THE FUTURE; 9. BLACK SWAN; 10. ALIEN.* **ROBIN AND THE MERRY MEN ANSWERS:** *1. A FOX; 2. LITTLE JOHN; 3. MARY ELIZABETH MASTRANTONIO; 4. SHERIFF OF NOTTINGHAM; 5. NOTTINGHAMSHIRE; 6. FRIAR TUCK; 7. ALLAN-A-DALE; 8. SAM BASS; 9. RICHARD GREENE; 10. ERROL FLYNN.*

THE MANY FACES OF SIR DAVID JASON

Just 5 of the many roles. Name the character and the TV shows

SHOWSTOPPERS

Which well-known musicals feature these songs:

1. Bring Him Home
2. Let's Go Fly A Kite
3. All That Jazz
4. Love Changes Everything
5. You'll Never Walk Alone
6. Sixteen Going on Seventeen
8. The Sun Has Got His Hat On
9. There's No Business Like Show Business
10. Oh, What A Beautiful Mornin'

MISSING LINK 6

What goes in the fourth box?

THE MANY FACES OF SIR DAVID JASON ANSWERS: *1. POP LARKIN, (DARLING BUDS OF MAY); 2.SHORTY MEPSTEAD, (LUCKY FELLER); 3. BLANCO, (PORRIDGE); 4. SKULLION, (PORTERHOUSE BLUE); 5. GRANVILLE, (STILL OPEN ALL HOURS).* **SHOWSTOPPERS ANSWERS:** *1. LES MISERABLES; 2. MARY POPPINS; 3. CHICAGO; 4. ASPECTS OF LOVE; 5. CAROUSEL; 6. THE SOUND OF MUSIC; 7. WEST SIDE STORY; 8. ME AND MY GIRL; 9. ANNIE GET YOUR GUN; 10. OKLAHOMA.* **– MISSING LINK6 ANSWER:** *NONE. This little piggy went to market, this little piggy stayed home, this little piggy had roast beef, this little piggy had none (and this little piggy cried wee wee wee all the way home.*

ONE LETTER ONLY

Can't get much simpler! Just one letter for each answer

1. Name the character who supplies James Bond with his gadgets?

2. What is the series of vitamins that includes niacin, riboflavin and thiamine.

3. The first person pronoun and ninth letter of the alphabet.

4. MPAA rating for films suitable for ages 17 and up

5. In sheet music, a letter that means 'soft'.

6. What is 500 in Roman numerals?

7. Three of these in a row indicates the sound of sleeping!

8. Tommy Lee Jones' character in the *Men in Black* was called Agent what?

9. An American TV sci-fi series in which aliens tried to gain control of Earth.

10. Which letter is represented by a single dot in Morse Code?

WHAT YEAR?

5 clues to guess a particular year. Points diminish with each clue.

5 POINTS. Michael Jackson became a father to a son.
Carlos the Jackal convicted.

4 POINTS. Pete Sampras and Martina Hingis won the titles at Wimbledon.
Landslide for Blair.

3 POINTS. Gianni Versace murdered.
Harry Potter and the Philosopher's Stone was a bestseller.

2 POINTS. Hong Kong returns to Chinese rule.
Hale Bopp was orbiting the Earth.

1 POINT. Diana, Princess of Wales and Mother Teresa died.
The movie *Titanic* was released.

ONE LETTER ONLY ANSWERS: 1. Q; 2. B; 3. I; 4. R; 5. P; 6. D; 7. Z; 8. K; 9. V; 10. E.
WHAT YEAR ANSWERS: *1997.*

WHAT THE DICKENS?
The great Charles from Victorian times

1. In what Charles Dickens novel does Mr. Wilkins Micawber appear?

2. Which English era was covered by most of Charles Dickens works?

3. Which antagonist led the team of pickpockets in the novel *Oliver Twist*?

4. Who is the hero of *Great Expectations*?

5. Of which newspaper was Dickens the founder-editor in 1846?

6. Which extremely mean character was reformed in *A Christmas Carol*?

7. Which novel starts: 'It was the best of times; it was the worst of times'?

8. In which year was Dickens born?   A) 1802   B) 1812   C) 1862   D) 1912

9. Where was Charles Dickens born?

10. Which Dickens heroine was born and raised in a debtors' prison?

WE DON'T ONLY ASK THE QUESTIONS!
Versatile people these quiz presenters!

1. Which game show host released his first novel, *The Thursday Murder Club* in 2020, and saw it become a long-standing number one best seller?

2. Which versatile TV actress succeeded Warwick Davis as host of *Tenable*?

3. Name the BBC newsreader who quizzes people in the *Mastermind* chair?

4. In 2021, which H.E. Bates character is Bradley Walsh playing?

5. Which world-renowned poker player hosts *Only Connect* on BBC2?

MAKE THE CONNECTION 8
4 people. What is the link?

WHAT THE DICKENS ANSWERS: *1. DAVID COPPERFIELD; 2. VICTORIAN; 3. FAGIN; 4. PIP; 5. THE DAILY NEWS; 6. EBENEZER SCROOGE; 7. A TALE OF TWO CITIES; 8. B) 1812; 9. PORTSMOUTH; 10. AMY DORRIT.* **WE DON'T ONLY ASK THE QUESTIONS! ANSWERS:** *1. RICHARD OSMAN; 2. SALLY LINDSAY; 3. CLIVE MYRIE; 4. POP LARKIN (in The Larkins); 5. VICTORIA COREN MITCHELL.* **MAKE THE CONNECTION 7 ANSWERS:** *ARMSTRONG. Alexander, Louis, Lance, Neil.*

MISCELLANY
A bit of everything

1. What links Mae West, David Livingstone, Stan Laurel and Marlene Dietrich?

2. What are 'Our Men', 'Our Ships at Sea' and 'A Willing Foe and Sea Room'?

3. What are 'Go deliver a dare, vile dog' and 'Norma is as selfless as I am Ron'?

4. What would a rock concert rate in decibels?   A) 70   B) 90   C) 110

5. What senior post in the Royal Households of the UK has been held by Martin Rees, Baron Rees of Ludlow, since 1995?

6. What title has been held by William Wordsworth, John Dryden, Robert Southey, Carol Ann Duffy and currently Simon Armitage?

7. What dish is a fillet steak wrapped in puff pastry?

8. In naval time keeping what watch is covered between 18:00 and 20:00?

9. What is the meaning of the ballet term Saut?

10. What familiar name given to Haydn's Symphony 94 in G, derives from the sudden loud chord played by the entire orchestra in the second movement?

ASSASSINATIONS
Who was the unfortunate victim for each set of clues below?

1. Shot by actor John Wilkes Booth in Ford's Theatre, Washington in 1865.

2. Murdered by four knights in Canterbury Cathedral in 1170.

3. Murdered with an ice pick whilst in exile in Mexico in 1940.

4. Murdered by members of her Sikh bodyguard in New Delhi in 1984.

5. Russian dissident poisoned by radionuclide polonium-210 in London, 2006

MISCELLANY ANSWERS: *1. ALL ON THE COVER OF THE BEATLES SGT PEPPER'S LONELY-HEARTS CLUB BAND; 2. ALL TOASTS OF THE NAVY; 3. PALINDROMES; 4. C) 110; 5. ASTRONOMERS ROYAL; 6. POETS LAUREATE; 7. BEEF WELLINGTON (Named in honour of the Duke of Wellington); 8. FIRST DOG WATCH; 9. A JUMP OFF BOTH FEET LANDING IN THE SAME POSITION; 10. THE SURPRISE.* **ASSASSINATIONS ANSWERS:** *1. ABRAHAM LINCOLN; 2. THOMAS BECKET; 3. LEON TROTSKY; 4. INDIRA GANDHI; 5. ALEXANDER LITVINENKO.*

STAND UP AND SAY THAT!

10 comedians to name from somewhat disguised pictures

MAKE YOUR CHOICE

Make your selection, A,B,C or D

1. At what age did Jimi Hendrix, Janis Joplin and Amy Winehouse all die?
A) 26   B) 27   C) 29   D) 30

2. What is Harry Potter's pet owl called?
A) Hedwig   B) Luna   C) Dobby   D) Fluffy

3. How often does the moon orbit the earth?
A) Every 7 days   B) Every 30 days   C) Every 365 days   D) Every 27 days

4. *The Da Vinci Code* film opens with a murder in which museum?
A) Guggenheim   B) Louvre   C) Van Gogh   D) Metropolitan Museum of Art

5. In 1896 the first person fined for speeding, Walter Arnold of East Peckham, was travelling at what speed?   A) 24mph   B) 8mph   C) 33mph   D) 12mph

6. As of June 2020, what is the highest recorded temperature recorded in the UK, and where was it?   A) 38.1°C - Kew Gardens   B) 37.4°C - Heathrow
C) 38.7°C – Cambridge   D) 39.8°C Enfield

7. Approximately how many cups of tea are drunk on a typical day in the UK?
A) 239,000   B) 88,000   C) 12 million   D) 165 million

8. The approximate average life expectancy in the UK in 1900 was 47. What was it in 2020?   A) 80   B) 72   C) 68   D) 66

9. What is FIFA's regulation circumference for a football in a professional or international match?   A) 38/40cm   B) 48/50cm   C) 68/70cm   D) 98/100cm

10. Diana Ross's 1970 debut solo single was called *Reach Out and Touch Somebody's ....?*   A) Face   B) Heart   C) Hand   D) Private parts

ZOOM IN

4 everyday objects pictured macro style in black and white. What are they?

MAKE YOUR CHOICE ANSWERS: *1. B) 27; 2. A) HEDWIG; 3. D) EVERY 27 DAYS; 4. B) LOUVRE; 5. B) 8MPH; 6. C) 38.7 AT CAMBRIDGE ON 25 JULY 2019; 7. D) 165 MILLION; 8. A) 80; 9. C) 68/70cm; 10. C) HAND.* **ZOOM IN ANSWERS:** *1. CORK; 2. APPLE STEM; 3. MATCHSTICK; 4. CRUNCHY NUT CORN FLAKES.*

SITTIN' IN THE BACK ROW
Film questions

1. The character Sonny Corleone was in which sequence of movies?

2. In which decade was *Rain Man* released?

3. In which Yorkshire steel city was *The Full Monty* set?

4. Who found fame as Charles in *Four Weddings and a Funeral*?

5. Which British studio was famous for producing horror films often starring Christopher Lee and Peter Cushing?

6. In the 1993 animated film *Aladdin*, which character did Robin Williams voice?

7. Walt Disney's *Bambi* was first released in: A) 1932   B) 1942   C) 1952?

8. Russell Crowe turned down the role of which protagonist in Peter Jackson's *Lord of the Rings* trilogy?

9. Who became the first woman to win a Best Director Oscar in 2010?

10. Who replaced Richard Harris as Dumbledore in the *Harry Potter* films?

WHERE IN THE WORLD?
5 clues to name a country. Less points as clues are taken

5 POINTS. This country had a population over 32 million in 2018. The flag is red and white.

4 POINTS. Fujimoristas, have caused political turmoil for any opposing faction in power.

3 POINTS. 3 official languages, Spanish, Aymara & Quechua. The Andes run length of country.

2 POINTS. Conquered in 16th century by Francisco Pizarro, Inca civilisation previously dominant.

1 POINT. South American country, coastline on the Pacific. Capital Lima. Paddington's homeland.

 **TRIVIAtime**

What's the maximum number of people that can play a game of Mouse Trap A) 2 B) 4 C) 6

SITTIN' IN THE BACK ROW ANSWERS: 1. THE GODFATHER; 2. 1980s;
3. SHEFFIELD; 4. HUGH GRANT; 5. HAMMER; 6. THE GENIE; 7. B) 1942;
8. ARAGORN; 9. KATHRYN BIGELOW; 10. MICHAEL GAMBON.
WHERE IN THE WORLD ANSWER: *PERU.* ***TRIVIAtime ANSWER:*** *B)4.*

SPORTING CHALLENGE

For the athletic quizzers!

1. In cricket, what is the umpire signalling with both hands pointed up in the air?

2. Where is the 2023 Rugby World Cup being held?

3. In what year were the Commonwealth Games first held?

4. What does NASCAR stand for?

5. In which city does the Tour de France finish?

6. Which London football club is farthest south, Arsenal or Chelsea?

7. How many players are there in a men's lacrosse team?

8. In netball, the abbreviation 'WA' refers to which position?

9. Who did Uruguay beat in the first-ever FIFA World Cup final?

10. David Beckham joined which team when he left Manchester United?

QUEUE FOR THE LADIES

There is a Lady in every answer

1. Which Paul McCartney composition, a piano led number one by The Beatles in 1968, saw them return to their rock 'n' roll roots?

2. What was the name of the yacht from which Robert Maxwell fell to his death?

3. Which song about his wife took Chris De Burgh to number one in 1986?

4. Which small, black spotted beetles are useful insects, because many of the 350 species prey on aphids and scale insects?

5. How is singer and actress Stefani Joanne Angelina Germanotta familiarly known?

6. Who rode through the streets of Coventry, in memorable fashion, to gain a remission of the oppressive taxation that her husband, Leofric, had imposed on his tenants?

7. Which 1955 Disney animated film features dogs called Jock, Trusty and Fluffy?

8. Name the lyrical ballad by the English poet Alfred Tennyson, which is based on the medieval La Damigella di Scalot, telling the story of Elaine of Astolat.

9. Who was an American socialite, and First Lady of the United States, from 1963 to 1969, as wife of 36th President of the United States?

10. Name the only daughter of Princess Margaret and Antony Armstrong-Jones, niece of Queen Elizabeth II, and the youngest grandchild of King George VI and Queen Elizabeth The Queen Mother.

SPORTING CHALLENGE ANSWERS: *1. A SIX; 2. FRANCE; 3. 1930; 4. National Association for Stock Car Auto Racing; 5. PARIS; 6. CHELSEA; 7. 10; 8. WING ATTACK; 9. ARGENTINA; 10. REAL MADRID.* **QUEUE FOR THE LADIES ANSWERS:** *1. LADY MADONNA; 2. LADY GHISLAINE; 3. LADY IN RED; 4. LADYBIRDS; 5. LADY GAGA; 6. LADY GODIVA; 7. THE LADY AND THE TRAMP; 8. THE LADY OF SHALLOT; 9. LADY BIRD JOHNSON; 10. LADY SARAH CHATTO.*

FAIRY TALES
The World of Hans Christian Andersen

1. Into what did the Ugly Duckling develop?

2. Andersen fell in love with the singer known as Swedish Nightingale in 1843. What was her name?

3. Who played the title role in the 1952 film *Hans Christian Andersen*?

4. In which Danish city was Hans born?

5. What is the name of the *Little Mermaid*?

6. There are 9 volumes of Andersen's Fairy Tales. How many stories?
A) 56   B) 126   C) 156

7. In *The Red Shoes* what can the shoes magically do?

8. Where in New York is there a statue of Andersen and the Ugly Duckling?

9. Which famous English author did Andersen befriend and visit on more than one occasion?

10. In *The Emperor's New Clothes* who is the first person to shatter the pretence of the tailors' lies?

PRIME MINISTERS QUESTION TIME
5 UK Prime Ministers in younger days. Name them.

FAIRY TALES ANSWERS: *1. A BEAUTIFUL SWAN; 2. JENNY LIND; 3. DANNY KAYE; 4. ODENSE; 5. ARIEL; 6. C) 156; 7. DANCE; 8. CENTRAL PARK; 9. CHARLES DICKENS; 10. A LITTLE BOY.*
MINISTERS QUESTION TIME ANSWERS: *1. HAROLD WILSON; 2. MARGARET THATCHER; 3. DAVID CAMERON; 4. THERESA MAY; 5. TONY BLAIR.*

ASSORTMENT
Another mixed bag

1. Who has been the First Minister of Wales since December 2018?

2. By landmass, what is the largest country in the world?

3. Prince changed his name to 'The Artist Formerly Known as Prince', or simply 'The Artist', or just a Symbol, but what was his real full name?

4. Which female comedy star and writer sang "Not bleakly, not meekly, Beat me on the bottom with a Woman's Weekly", sadly died, aged 62, in 2016?

5. Which British alt-rock band won the 2018 Mercury Prize for their second album *Visions of a Life*?

6. Name the serial killer played by Jodie Comer in hit series *Killing Eve*?

7. Which actor plays Dr. Ivo Robotnik in the *Sonic the Hedgehog* movie?

8. In 2018 which country became the first major industrialised country to legalise cannabis?

9. Which country hosted the 2018 Winter Olympic Games?

10. Which author wrote the dystopian novel *The Handmaid's Tale*?

BUILDER UPPER
Name the 8 people pictured and find a connection between the pictures

Who was Henry VIIIs last wife?

POT POURRI
How wide is your knowledge?

1. In which year did the Scots defeat the English at Bannockburn?

2. In a street of 100 consecutively numbered houses (1-100), how many number nines are used?

3. What cost 37p when it was abolished in 1988?

4. Adrenaline is produced by the adrenal glands located where in the body?

5. What type of car is associated with Lady Penelope Creighton-Ward?

6. What vegetable includes the following varieties: Burpless Tasty Green; Tokyo Green; Muncher?

7. At which famous location was George Mallory's body found in 1999; 75 years after his death?

8. What links the death of Henry V with telephone caller identification?

9. What can go up a chimney down but not down a chimney up?

10. Name the occupation. Is it a Walsall FC player?

BIRDS EYE UK
6 landmarks to identify from above

POT POURRI ANSWERS: *1. 1314; 2. 20; 3. DOG LICENCE; 4. ADJACENT TO THE KIDNEYS; 5. (A PINK) ROLLS ROYCE; 6. CUCUMBER; 7. MOUNT EVEREST; 8. 1471; 9. AN UMBRELLA; 10. A SADDLER.*
BIRDS EYE U.K. ANSWERS: *1. ASHTON GATE, BRISTOL; 2. THE GHERKIN, LONDON; 3. THE MAZE, HAMPTON COURT PALACE; STONEHENGE; 4. SKOMER ISLAND; 5. ST. PAUL'S CATHEDRAL.*

LET'S HAVE A MOMENT OF SCIENCE!

A study of the structure and behaviour of the physical and natural world

1. What disease killed more people in 1918 than died in the First World War?

2. The orbit of which planet takes it farthest from the Sun?

3. What is another name for your sternum?

4. What name is given to the process by which yeast converts into sugar?

5. Microwave, infrared, visible, ultraviolet…. What comes next?

6. Who said: "Science without religion is lame, religion without science is blind"?

7. What single word was the first ever to be reproduced on a photocopier?
A) Xerox   B) Astoria   C) Carlson   D) Supercaliflawjalisticexpialidoshus

8. Which pair of Cambridge scientists unravelled the structure of DNA and won the Nobel Prize in Medicine in 1962?

9. What is thought to have been created in the Big Bang?

10. What does a Bessemer Converter produce?

WHAT AM I?

The quicker you guess, the more points you get!

5 POINTS - *I am the setting for Three Men and a Boat*

4 POINTS - *I used to occupy The Strand*

3 POINTS - *I have two banks of my own*

2 POINTS - *I am 210 miles long*

1 POINT - *You'll find Cleopatra's Needle on my left side*

SPOT THE LINK

Look at the four pictures below and find a connection.

LET'S HAVE A MOMENT OF SCIENCE! ANSWERS: 1. INFLUENZA; 2. PLUTO; 3. BREASTBONE; 4. FERMENTATION; 5. X-RAY (On the electromagnetic spectrum); 6. ALBERT EINSTEIN; 7. B) ASTORIA (The hotel where Carlson stayed whilst inventing Xerox); 8. Francis Crick and James Watson; 9. EVERYTHING! (Believed to have been the moment the universe began); 10. STEEL. *WHAT AM I? ANSWER:* THE RIVER THAMES. *SPOT THE LINK ANSWER: BIRDS -* Jack SPARROW, CRANE, ROBIN, Clarice STARLING.

MOVIE MAGIC

Film time!

1. Which part is voiced by John Lithgow in *Shrek*?

2. In Harry Potter and the Deathly Hallows, Charlie reveals to Hagrid that Norbert is female and had been renamed Norberta. What breed of dragon is Norberta?

3. Who is Darth Vader's mother?

4. Julianne Moore played FBI agent Clarice Starling in:
A) Which film   B) Who had played her in an earlier movie?

5. In the 1989 film *Turner and Hooch*, what was Tom Hanks' slobbery partner?

6. Which famous aviator's story was told in the 1957 film *The Spirit of St Louis*?

7. To what did Bristolian Archibald Leach change his name to find fame?

8. How many Von Trapp children featured in *The Sound of Music* in 1965?

9. In the 1994 film *Mary Shelley's Frankenstein*, Kenneth Branagh played Victor Frankenstein. Who played the product of his experiment with corpses and electricity?

10. Who plays Ripley in Alien, Aliens, Alien 3 and Alien: Resurrection?

CAN'T SEE THE WOOD FOR THE TREES

Identify the trees from their botanical names

1. *Corylus avellana*

2. *Taxus baccata*

3. *Ilex aquifolium*

4. *Quercus*

5. *Ulmus minor*

6. *Salix babylonica*

7. *Sorbus aucuparia*

8. *Picea abies*

9. *Fagus sylvatica*

10. *Cedrus*

MOVIE MAGIC ANSWERS: *1. LORD FARQUAAD; 2. NORWEGIAN RIDGEBACK; 3. SHMI SKYWALKER; 4. A) HANNIBAL, B) JODIE FOSTER (in Silence of the Lambs); 5. BORDEAUX MASTIFF DOG; 6. CHARLES LINDBERGH; 7. CARY GRANT; 8. SEVEN; 9. ROBERT DE NIRO; 10. SIGOURNEY WEAVER.*
CAN'T SEE THE WOOD FOR THE TREES ANSWERS: *1. HAZEL; 2. YEW; 3. HOLLY; 4. OAK; 5. ELM; 6. WEEPING WILLOW; 7. ROWAN (or Mountain ash); 8. NORWAY SPRUCE; 9. COMMON BEECH; 10. CEDAR.*

ANTIQUES ROADSHOW

Can you value these items as seen on the TV show?

CAN YOU CORRECTLY
VALUE ALL OF
THESE ITEMS?

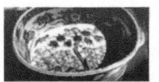

1. The previous owner had used this 17th century dish as a dog bowl?
1. £1 B) £10
C) £2,500 D) £35,000

2. Top-secret documents with previously unknown code-words for D-Day landings?
1. £1,000 B) £10,000
C) £100,000 D) £35,000

3. A Clash T-shirt. Expert was excited but said it was low quality fabric.
1. £1 B) £100
C) £450 D) £22,500

4. Tombola from Grand Hotel at time of the 1984 IRA Brighton bombing. Raffle tickets for Tory cabinet inside.
1. £200 B) £5,000
C) £18,000 D) £0

5. Brass mounted clock? Made 1760, plays delightful music on hour. Big demand in China for such clocks.
1. £10 B) £500
C) £1,000 D) £15,000

6. Paperweight owned by Winston Churchill during World War II.
1. £1 B) £50
C) £500 D) £112,000

7. Signed painting, by Charles Dixon, showing Thames 1920? Found in skip.
1. £3,000 B) £6,000
C) £18,000 D) £300,000

8. Monopoly played in farmhouse b, The Great Train Robbers in 1963?
1. £100 B) £120
C) £4,000 D) £16,000

9. Simon & Halbig, a huge German maker of dolls, much valued by expert
1.80 B) £150
C) £10,000 D) £150,000

10. Finally, this "Angel of the North" Gormley sculpture, used to convince Newcastle council to build the big one.
1. £1,000 B) £23,000
C) £75,000 D) £1 million

ANTIQUES ROADSHOW ANSWERS: 1. C) £2500; 2. A) £1,000; 3. C) £450; 4. B) £5,000; 5. D) £15,000; 6. C) £500; 7. A) £3,000; 8. A) £100; 9. C) £10,000; 10. D) £1m.

BACK IN TIME
Back to times of old

1. Which Scottish clan, often accused of collusion with the English, murdered members of the MacDonald clan in The Massacre of Glencoe in 1692?

2. At the outbreak of the First World War who was the Prime Minister?

3. Who was the first person to reach the South Pole in 1911?

4. On which day of the week did Christopher Columbus discover Dominica in November 1493 whilst sailing for Spain?

5. In which maritime fire disaster did 167 men lose their lives 120 miles off the Scottish coast in July 1988?

6. Cleopatra had four children. Name the two men who fathered them.

7. How many people went aboard Noah's Ark?

8. What instrument did bandleader Glenn Miller play?

9. What technical innovation did Sony invent in 1979?

10. What eye-catching building, completed in 1648, contains the tomb of Queen Mumtaz Mahal?

CHARACTERS IN LITERATURE
Match the character with the book in which they appear

1. SAM WELLER	a. BREAKFAST AT TIFFANY'S
2. WILLY LOMAN	b. KING SOLOMON'S MINES
3. MISS HAVISHAM	c. PRIDE AND PREDUJICE
4. HUMBERT HUMBERT	d. VANITY FAIR
5. SEBASTIAN FLYTE	e. PICKWICK PAPERS
6. ALLAN QUATERMAIN	f. FAR FROM THE MADDING CROWD
7. HOLLY GOLIGHTLY	g. GREAT EXPECTATIONS
8. BATHSHEBA EVERDENE	h. LOLITA
9. BECKY SHARP	j. DEATH OF A SALESMAN
10. ELIZABETH BENNETT	k. BRIDESHEAD REVISITED

BACK IN TIME ANSWERS: *1. CAMPBELLS; 2. HERBERT ASQUITH; 3. ROALD AMUNDSEN; 4. SUNDAY (Domingo is Sunday in Spanish); 5. PIPER ALPHA OIL PLATFORM; 6. JULIUS CAESAR AND MARK ANTONY; 7. EIGHT; 8. TROMBONE; 9. SONY WALKMAN; 10. THE TAJ MAHAL.*
CHARACTERS IN LITERATURE ANSWERS: *1e, 2j, 3g, 4h, 5k, 6b, 7a, 8f, 9d, 10c.*

WHAT YEAR?

Some events are listed. In which year did they occur?

1. Jeffrey Archer jailed for perjury; Foot-and-Mouth disease breaks out in the UK; 9/11 terrorist attacks on the World Trade Center; Apple release the iPod; George W Bush elected as president.

2. Yuri Gagarin first man in space; John F Kennedy becomes US President; Berlin Wall is erected; UN secretary Daj Hammarskjöld is killed in an air crash.

3. Britain joins EEC; 3-day working week declared; Richard Nixon elected for second term as US president; The Godfather gets Best Picture Oscar; Arad oil producers blockade oil supplies.

4. Terry Waite taken hostage in Lebanon; Herald of Free Enterprise capsizes and 193 people die; Lester Piggot jailed for tax evasion; Coventry City win FA Cup for the first time in their history.

5. Good Friday Agreement signed in Northern Ireland; Bill Clinton and Monica Lewinsky!; France beat Brazil 3-0 to win World Cup; Titanic wins 11 Oscars.

6. Dalai Lama forced to flee Tibet; Hawaii and Alaska join United States; Fidel Castro seizes power in Cuba; The first section of motorway (M1) is opened.

7. Hong Kong falls to the Japanese; The Bismarck sunk by the Royal Navy; Penicillin used for the first time; Japanese bomb US naval base Pearl Harbor.

8. Suffragette Emily Davison killed at the Derby; senators to be elected for the first time in the US; First ever crossword is published in New York World. Attempt to sell the stolen Mona Lisa.

9. Winter Olympics held in Lillehammer; First female priests ordained in the Anglican church; Nelson Mandela becomes South Africa president; the Channel Tunnel opens. Ayrton Senna killed.

10. San Francisco destroyed by severe earthquake; Simplon Tunnel is opened; SOS becomes international distress signal; Rolls-Royce is founded.

MISSING LANDMARKS

Can you work out which famous landmarks have been airbrushed out?

WHAT YEAR? ANSWERS: *1. 2001; 2. 1961; 3. 1973; 4. 1987; 5. 1998; 6. 1959; 7. 1941; 8. 1913; 9. 1994; 10. 1906.* **MISSING LANDMARKS ANSWERS:** *BIG BEN, LONDON; STATUE OF LIBERTY, NEW YORK; TAJ MAHAL, AGRA; SYDNEY OPERA HOUSE (Shown on next page).*

MUSICAL INTERLUDE
Popular music of several shades

1. What is the name of the garden of remembrance for John Lennon in Central Park?

2. Who founded the Proms concerts, first held in London in 1895?

3. Which singer was born in Rochdale in 1898 and died on the island of Capri in 1979?

4. Despite being unrelated, under what name did Scott Engel, Gary Leeds and John Maus have a string of hits in the UK between 1965 and 1975?

5. Which funk and soul band did Lionel Richie leave to pursue a solo career in 1982?

6. What instrument accompanies a piano, a violin and a viola in a piano quartet?

7. What is the name of country music singing star Loretta Lynn's sister?

8. The seafaring opera *Billy Budd* was based upon a story by which author?

9. Which famous film director got to No. 12 in the UK charts in 1984 with *To Be or Not to Be (The Hitler Rap)*?

10. Who composed the *Blue Danube Waltz*?

ANAGRAM TIME
Solve the anagram!
ORIENT HITS QUIZ (3,11)

MISSING LANDMARKS ANSWERS
From the previous page

MUSICAL INTERLUDE ANSWERS: *1. STRAWBERRY FIELDS; 2. SIR HENRY WOOD; 3. GRACIE FIELDS; 4. THE WALKER BROTHERS; 5. THE COMMODORES; 6. CELLO; 7. CRYSTAL GAYLE; 8. HERMAN MELVILLE; 9. MEL BROOKS; 10. JOHANN STRAUSS.* **ANAGRAM TIME ANSWER:** *THE INQUIZITORS.*

I-N-Q-U-I-Z-I-T-O-R

*The **initial** letters to each question spell the word Inquizitor*

1. What **I** is dyspepsia more commonly known as?

2. What **N** is the fur of the coypu?

3. What **Q** is the equivalent of half a crotchet?

4. Which **U** is a 9-letter word meaning a final offer of terms?

5. If 25 equals silver and 50 equals gold, what **I** equals 14?

6. What **Z** was given to French foot soldiers wearing Arab dress?

7. In which **I** sport is The Stanley Cup a major competition?

8. What **T** is a spice used to colour curry yellow?

9. What **O** do coin collectors call the head side of a coin?

10. Which **R** were a Swedish duo who had a 1991 hit with *Joyride*?

LONDON'S ROYAL PARKS

There are 8 of them, covering 4,900 acres. Can you name them?

MORTICIA ADDAMS

What was Morticia's maiden name? Name the actresses (above) who have played her on screen?

NAME THAT SONG

We give you the opening line, you name the singer and the song

1. At first I was afraid, I was petrified.

2. There is a lady who's sure all that glitters is gold.

3. Knew he was a killer first time that I saw him, wonder how many girls he had loved and left haunted.

4. And now, the end is near, and so I face the final curtain.

5. Son, I'm 30, I only went with your mother cos she's dirty.

6. Once upon a time you dressed so fine, threw the bums a dime in your prime, didn't you?

7. I've had nothing but bad luck since the day I saw the cat at my door.

8. I know that I can't keep her now she's in love with you.

9. Don't think I can't feel that there's something wrong, you've been the sweetest part of my life for so long.

10. You took a mystery and made me want it, you got a pedestal and put me on it.

SONG TITLES PICTURE DINGBATS
Title and the artistes please!

ROxxW

ROW

ROW

A

B

T
O
W
N

C

BRAIN TESTERS

All sorts

1. In what famous building would you find the Hall of Mirrors?

2. What is the cheapest property on the London version of Monopoly ?

3. Who ended each episode of *The Magic Roundabout* with 'Time for bed'?

4. Who is the only British Prime Minister to marry a divorcee?

5. Who sculpted *The Kiss*?

6. Who wears the *Fisherman's Ring*?

7. What connects the discoverer of penicillin and the creator of James Bond?

8. Arch, girder, cantilever and suspension are all types of what?

9. What type of confectionery has a name that literally means 'baked twice'?

10. What was the scarecrow lacking in the *Wizard of Oz*?

KIDDIES KORNER!

The children might know these answers

1. Who told the Queen that Snow White was 'the fairest of them all'?

2. What would you store in MP3 format on your computer?

3. In Scrabble what is the value of the blank tile?

4. In which town does Noddy live?

5. In which garden did Adam and Eve live?

6. Who met three bears in a fairy-tale?

7. Who is the oldest of the seven dwarfs?

8. Which famous highwayman rode a horse called Black Bess?

9. In the initials RSPCA, what does the P stand for?

10. What does Spiderman shoot from his wrists to capture criminals?

BRAIN TESTERS ANSWERS: *1. PALACE OF VERSAILLES; 2. OLD KENT ROAD (£60); 3. ZEBEDEEE; 4. MARGARET THATCHER; 5. AUGUSTE RODIN; 6. THE POPE; 7. FLEMING (Alexander and Ian); 8. BRIDGES; 9.BISCUIT; 10. A BRAIN.*
KIDDIES KORNER! ANSWERS: *1. THE MAGIC MIRROR; 2. AUDIO; 3. ZERO; 4. TOYTOWN; 5. GARDEN OF EDEN; 6. GOLDILOCKS; 7. DOC; 8. DICK TURPIN; 9. PREVENTION; 10. STICKY WEBS.*

A PORTION OF PORRIDGE

A test on the wonderful sit-com starring Ronnie Barker from 1973-1977

1. What is Norman Fletcher's middle name?

2. Lennie Godber was in prison for burglary. How was he caught?

3. In *Just Desserts*, what sort of tinned fruit disappeared?

4. Fulton Mackay played Mr. Mackay. What was the warder's first name?

5. How many children does Fletcher have?

6. In the opening credits the judge says "You are an habitual criminal, who accepts arrest as ………? Can you finish the sentence?

7. Fletcher and Blanco fooled Norris into believing that there was £8,000 buried where?

8. Which of the inmates stages a rooftop protest to help Fletcher get back in the Governor's good books?

9. What was the name of the prison where Fletcher was sent to do Porridge?

10. Brian Wilde played Mr. Barraclough? He also starred in 116 episodes of *Last of the Summer Wine* and as Bloody Delilah in what other TV sit-com?

CATCHPHRASES

Name the people or characters that gave us these sayings on TV

1. Computer says no"

2. 'Zoinks'

3. 'Garlic bread'.

4. 'I didn't get where I am today….'

5. 'You dirty old man'

6. 'You're my wife now'

7. 'Does my bum look big in this?'

8. It's good but it's not right'

9. 'Whaddya gonna do?

10. 'Three words: Fab-u-LOUS!'

A PORTION OF PORRIDGE ANSWERS: 1. STANLEY; 2. HE GOT STUCK IN A CHIMNEY; 3. PINEAPPLE CHUNKS; 4. IT WAS NEVER REVEALED; 5. 3 (Ingrid, Raymond & Marion); 6. OCCUPATIONAL HAZARD; 7. UNDER THE PITCH AT ELLAND ROAD (Leeds United FC); 8. McLAREN; 9. SLADE PRISON; 10. THE DUSTBINMEN. **CATCHPHRASES ANSWERS:** 1. Carol Beer (Little Britain); 2. Shaggy (Scooby Doo); 3. Brian Potter (Phoenix Nights); 4. C.J. (Reginald Perrin); 5. Harold Steptoe (Steptoe & Son); 6. Papa Lazarou (League of Gentlemen); 7. Arabella Weir (The Fast Show); 8. Roy Walker (Catchphrase); 9. Tony Soprano (The Sopranos); 10. Craig Revel Horwood (Strictly Come Dancing).

LET THERE BE DRUMS

How many top percussionists can you name? Spot a link between numbers 10 & 11 too!

LET THERE BE DRUMS ANSWERS: 1. BRIAN BENNETT; 2. CHARLIE WATTS; 3. CINDY BLACKMAN; 4. JOHN BONHAM; 5. KAREN CARPENTER; 6. KEITH MOON; 7. STEWART COPELAND; 8. PHIL COLLINS; 9. SHEILA E; 10. RINGO STARR; 11. ZAK STARKEY (Son of Ringo!); 12. GINGER BAKER; 13. NEIL PEART; 14. IAN PAICE; 15. MEG WHITE.

GREEN AND PLEASANT LAND

All around the UK

1. Which city has the nickname of the 'city of dreaming spires'?

2. Which village in Wales shares its name with a term meaning to 'say something indistinctly and quietly'?

3. The River Severn is the longest river in Britain at 220 miles (354 km), but which is the second longest?

4. What is 'The Boston Stump'?

5. What historic castle was built by William the Conqueror in 1078?

6. What county has held the title 'Garden of England' for over 400 years?

7. Which area, about 25 miles inland, is known as an island, because the surrounding fens were very marshy until 19th century drainage projects?

8. In 1840, which arboretum was the first public park in Britain?

9. What is the estimated percentage of green space coverage in Greater London?   A) 10%   B) 25%   C) 47%,   d) 60%

10. What is generally regarded as the first publicly funded park in the UK?

CHILDREN'S TALES OF THE UNEXPECTED

Roald Dahl wrote 18 children's stories. How many of them can you name?

GREEN AND PLEASANT LAND ANSWERS: *1. OXFORD; 2. MUMBLES; 3. RIVER THAMES; 4. 275ft high tower of St Botolph's church in Boston, Lincolnshire; 5. THE TOWER OF LONDON; 6. KENT; 7. ISLE OF ELY; 8. DERBY ARBORETUM; 9. C) 47%; 10. BIRKENHEAD PARK ON MERSEYSIDE.*

TALES OF THE UNEXPECTED ANSWERS: *– (in order of writing) The Gremlins, James and the Giant Peach, Charlie and the Chocolate Factory, The Magic Finger, Fantastic Mr Fox, Charlie and the Great Glass Elevator, Danny the Champion of the World, Wonderful Story of Henry Sugar and 6 more, The Enormous Crocodile, The Twits, George's Marvellous Medicine, The BFG, The Giraffe and the Pelly and Me, Matilda, Esio Trot, The Minpins, The Vicar of Nibbleswicke.*

BALL GAMES
A load of balls

1. What is the minimum number of players in a softball team?

2. What colour shirts are worn by the French Rugby Union national team?

3. What name is given to the fielding positions in cricket close behind the wicket on the offside?

4. Which American sport was invented by Abner Doubleday?

5. What nickname is given to the clubhouse on a golf course?

6. Which country won every Olympic men's hockey gold medal from 1928 to 1964?

7. In what game does a player shoot from a line called a taw?

8. Which sport is generally regarded as being the fastest ball game?

9. In which country was the sport of croquet invented?

10. Which team lost two consecutive FA Cup Finals in 1998 and 1999?

HOBBIES AND PROFESSIONS
What do you call the following?

1. One skilled in folding paper
2. A beekeeper
3. A bell ringer
4. One who makes barrels
5. A tree surgeon
6. A wine expert
7. A pork butcher
8. A collector of stamps
9. Someone who makes bells or castings
10. A maker of archery bows

BALL GAMES ANSWERS: *1. 9; 2. BLUE; 3. SLIPS; 4. BASEBALL; 5. THE 19th HOLE; 6. INDIA; 7. MARBLES; 8. PELOTA; 9. FRANCE; 10. NEWCASTLE UNITED.*
HOBBIES AND PROFESSIONS ANSWERS: *1. ORIGAMIST; 2. APIARIST; 3. CAMPANOLOGIST; 4. COOPER; 5. ARBORIST; 6. SOMMELIER; 7. CHARCUTIER; 8. PHILATELIST; 9. FOUNDER; 10. BOWYER*

IF MUSIC BE THE FOOD OF LOVE

Play on!

1. Who was backed by a band called The Blackhearts?

2. Errol Browne was the lead singer with which band?

3. Ed Sheeran's first album in 2011 was entitled which mathematical symbol?

4. *Devil Woman* was a hit for Cliff Richard in what year?
 A) 1956   B) 1966   C) 1976   D) 1986

5. Which member of The Eagles charted with *The Boys of Summer* in 1985?

6. Which country singer starred in the movies *9 to 5* and *Steel Magnolias*?

7. How many valves does a trumpet have?

8. Which song opens with the line, 'There is a house in New Orleans ?

9. What name is given to the principal female singer in an opera?

10. Who had hits with 'Sweet' songs?
A) Sweet Caroline   B) Sweet Nothin's   C) Sweet Soul Music

PLACE NAME MEANINGS

Name the places from the descriptions

1. Country meaning 'rich coast'
2. Caribbean town meaning 'rich harbour'
3. Mountain range meaning 'snowy range'
4. South American city meaning 'river of January'
5. Country meaning 'land of silver'
6. London district, named from a hunting cry
7. African city meaning 'lakes'
8. Indian state meaning 'land of kings'
9. Country meaning 'lion mountains'
10. US state meaning 'place of the gods'

HOW RUDE!

Who had the following nicknames?
A) TURNIP, B) SUPERBRAT, C) HAIRY CORNFLAKE, D) INTERESTING,
E) REFRIGERATOR F) MONKEY BOY G) STICKS H) COLLY J) MOUSEBOY

IF MUSIC BE THE FOOD OF LOVE ANSWERS: 1. JOAN JETT; 2. HOT CHOCOLATE; 3. +; 4. C) 1976; 5. DON HENLEY; 6. DOLLY PARTON; 7. THREE; 8. HOUSE OF THE RISING SUN (By The Animals); 9. PRIMA DONNA; 10. A) NEIL DIAMOND, B) BRENDA LEE, C) ARTHUR CONLEY. PLACE NAME MEANINGS ANSWERS: 1. COSTA RICA; 2. PUERTO RICA; 3. SIERRA NEVADA; 4. RIO DE JANEIRO; 5. ARGENTINA; 6. SOHO; 7. LAGOS; 8. RAJASTHAN; 9. SIERRA LEONE; 10. HAWAII. HOW RUDE ANSWERS: A) GRAHAM TAYLOR; B) JOHN McENROE; C) DAVE LEE TRAVIS; D) STEVE DAVIS; E) WILLIAM PERRY F) CHRIS PRATT; G) HUGH JACKMAN; H) OLIVIA COLMAN; J) RYAN GOSLING.

BLINDED BY SCIENCE?

Structure and behaviour of the physical and natural world

1. What animal has the largest eyes?

2. What is short for 'light amplification by stimulated emission of radiation'?

3. What do the initials USB stand for in computer science?

4. When can a sonic boom be heard?

5. What painkiller is connected to a cricket bat?

6. Where would you find a tungsten filament?

7. What sex is a person with XX chromosomes?

8. North of the Equator, which way does water swirl down the plughole?

9. Where in your body does hydrochloric acid occur naturally?

10. What is 'dry ice'?

FOOD FOR THOUGHT

A mouth-watering round

1. Name both ingredients of the savoury dish Devils on Horseback.

2. in what city did Sally Lunn sell teacakes that bear her name?

3. Which vegetable is known as zucchini in the USA?

4. Which fruit is a cross between a plum and a peach?

5.Which animal was originally used to produce mozzarella cheese?

6. Profiteroles and éclairs are made from which type of pastry?

7. Which of the following is NOT an ingredient of Worcestershire Sauce?
A) Tamarind   B) Anchovies   C) Molasses   D) Tomatoes

8. Which French city is known for the fish stew Bouillabaisse?
a) Marseille   b) Nice   c) Bordeaux   d) Paris

9. A Whitby Bun flavouring is:
A) Raspberry   B) Coffee   C) Cinnamon   D) Lemon

10. What is a Goosnargh cake?   A) A cake from Yorkshire   B) A biscuit from Lancashire   C) A cake from Wales   D) A biscuit from Kent

BLINDED BY SCIENCE? ANSWERS: *1. THE GIANT SQUID; 2. LASER; 3. UNIVERSAL SERIAL BUS; 4. WHEN THE SPEED OF SOUND IS SURPASSED; 5. ASPIRIN (from willow bark, cricket bat made of willow); 6. IN A LIGHT BULB; 7. FEMALE; 8. ANTI-CLOCKWISE; 9. IN YOUR STOMACH; 10. SOLID CARBON DIOXIDE (CO2).* **FOOD FOR THOUGHT ANSWERS:** *1. PRUNES AND BACON; 2. BATH; 3. COURGETTES; 4. NECTARINE; 5. BUFFALO; 6. CHOUX PASTRY; 7. D) TOMATOES; 8. A) MARSEILLES; 9. A) RASPBERRY; 10. B) A TYPE OF BISCUIT ORIGINATING IN LANCASHIRE (spiced with caraway seeds).*

BLUE MOVIES

The air was blue in these films

1. What was the title of the 2013 American dark comedy-drama film, written and directed by Woody Allen that tells the story of a rich Manhattan socialite who falls into hard times?

2. Name the 1961 American musical romantic comedy film set in the state of Hawaii and starring Elvis Presley.

3. Who played headmistress Miss Amelia Fritton in the 1957 comedy *Blue Murder at St. Trinians*?

4. Who sang the title song for the 1970 film *Soldier Blue*, a No. 7 hit?

5. What was the title of the 1966 war film, starring Ursula Andress and George Peppard, about a German fighter pilot on the Western Front during WW1?

6. Who sang *Falling in Love Again* in the 1930 film The Blue Angel ?

7. In the 1980 movie *The Blues Brothers*, who starred with John Belushi?

8. *Rhapsody in Blue* is a 1945 fictionalised screen biography of which American composer and musician?

9. In *Blue Velvet* (1986) what does a young student, visiting his sick father, discover in a field that leads to the uncovering of a vast criminal conspiracy?

10. What 1995 film is based on Walter Mosley's novel and features Denzel Washington as a WWII veteran, unfairly laid off from an aircraft manufacturer, and becoming a private investigator just to pay the mortgage?

RUBIK'S CUBE

What are the colours used in the original cube?

BLUE MOVIES ANSWERS: *1. BLUE JASMINE; 2. BLUE HAWAII; 3. ALASTAIR SIM; 4. BUFFY ST MARIE; 5. THE BLUE MAX; 6. MARLENE DIETRICH; 7. DAN AYKROYD; 8. GEORGE GERSHWIN; 9. A SEVERED HUMAN EAR; 10. DEVIL IN A BLUE DRESS.*
RUBIK'S CUBE ANSWERS: *RED, YELLOW, GREEN, BLUE, ORANGE, WHITE.*

TOMORROW'S CHIP PAPER

Newspaper round

1. *You* magazine is a women's magazine supplement in which newspaper?

2. What is the official news publication of The Salvation Army?

3. After 168 years, *The News of the World* printed its final edition in what year?

4. In February 2018 *The Sun's* 40-year domination at the top of the UK circulation charts was eclipsed by which newspaper?

5. Name the British daily horse racing, greyhound racing and sports betting publication launched in April 1986?

6. The Rupert Bear comic strip has appeared in which British daily newspaper since 1920?

7. Which columnist left *The Sun* to write for the *Daily Mail* and nowadays contributes an amusing, hard-hitting column which has earned him Columnist of the Year Awards?

8. Which British newspaper was founded in 1855 with the motto, "Was, is, and will be"? This motto continues in 2020 whilst sales have risen to 360,000.

9. What did Arthur Wynne invent in December 1913 for the Sunday newspaper, *New York World*?

10. The UK's first colour newspaper was launched in 1986 by Eddie Shah. It ran until 1995. What was its title?

DANCE THE NIGHT AWAY

Use the descriptions to identify the dances

1. Erotic dance, usually a striptease, performed in private to a seated person.

2. Rock and Roll dance of the 1960s popularised by Chubby Checker.

3. Folk dance usually in 6/8 time and particularly associated with Ireland.

4. European ballroom dance in ¾ time that emerged in Vienna in the 1780s.

5. 19th century Bohemian dance, comprising 3 steps and a hop to fast 2/4 time.

TOMORROW'S CHIP PAPER ANSWERS: 1. THE MAIL ON SUNDAY; 2. WAR CRY; 3. 2011; 4. METRO (a free paper); 5. RACING POST; 6. DAILY EXPRESS; 7. RICHARD LITTLEJOHN; 8. DAILY TELEGRAPH; 9. THE CROSSWORD PUZZLE; 10. TODAY. DANCE THE NIGHT AWAY ANSWERS: 1. LAP DANCE; 2. THE TWIST; 3. JIG; 4. WALTZ; 5. POLKA.

ANOTHER ARRAY

Last collection

1. How many children in Enid Blyton's "Famous Five"?

2. What colour is the neutral wire on a domestic plug?

3. What name is given to the study of fossils?

4. What colour is the cross on the flag of Denmark?

5. In which city would you find the Spanish Riding School?

6. How many pairs of ribs would a normal human have?

7. Which English city did the Romans call Deva?

8. In 1939 the UK's largest opera house was opened. In which town was it?

9. The musical Cats was based upon the poems of which poet?

10. Of what would you be afraid if you suffered from gametophobia?

WATCHING THE DETECTIVES

9 actors, 9 TV shows. Match them up!

1. SCOTT AND BAILEY	A. MARTIN SHAW
2. ENDEAVOUR	B. ASHLEY JENSEN
3. WALLANDER	C. BRENDA BLETHYN
4. A TOUCH OF FROST	D. DAVID JASON
5. FOYLE'S WAR	E. SHAUN EVANS
6. VERA	F. JOAN HICKSON
7. MISS MARPLE	G. PATRICIA ROUTLEDGE
8. INSPECTOR GEORGE GENTLY	H. MICHAEL KITCHEN
9. AGATHA RAISIN	J. SURANNE JONES
10. HETTY WAINTHROP INVESTIGATES	K. KENNETH BRANAGH

 **TRIVIAtime**

Which Oasis song opens with the lyrics 'Maybe I don't really wanna know / How your garden grows / 'Cause I just wanna fly'?

ANOTHER ARRAY ANSWERS: *1. FOUR (Timmy the dog made up the 5); 2. BLUE; PALAEOTOLOGY; 4. WHITE; 5. VIENNA; 6. 12; 7. CHESTER; 8. BLACKPOOL; 9. T S ELIOT; 10. MARRIAGE.* **WATCHING THE DETECTIVES ANSWERS:** *1J, 2E, 3K, 4D, 5H, 6C, 7F, 8A, 9B, 10G.* **TRIVIAtime ANSWER:** *LIVE FOREVER.*

JUST CAPITALS

Name the capital cities of the following countries:

1. Australia;
2. Portugal;
3. Turkey;
4. Tunisia;

5. Slovakia.

ADVERTISING SLOGANS

Identify the products associated with these words

1. 'Naughty but nice.
2. 'Let your fingers do the walking'.
3. 'Live well for less'.
4. 'Let's make things better'.
5. 'The longer-lasting snack.
6. 'Is she or isn't she?'.
7. 'Life's for sharing'.
8. 'You can't put a better bit of butter on your knife'.
9. 'The ultimate driving machine'.
10. 'We won't make a drama out of a crisis'.

DEM BONES, DEM BONES....

Where in the body would you find these bones?

1. FEMUR; 2. STERNUM;

3. CARPALS; 4. HUMERUS;

5. CLAVICLE; 6. TIBIA;

7. INCUS; 8. ULNA;

9. TALUS;

10. SCAPULA.

JUST CAPITALS ANSWERS: *1. CANBERRA; 2. LISBON; 3. ANKARA; 4. TUNIS; 5. BRATISLAVA.* **ADVERTISING SLOGANS ANSWERS:** *1. CREAM CAKES (NATIONAL DAIRY COUNCIL); 2. YELLOW PAGES; 3. SAINSBURY'S; 4. PHILIPS; 5. TWIX; 6. HARMONY HAIRSPRAY; 7. T-MOBILE; 8. COUNTRY LIFE BUTTER; 9. BMW; 10. COMMERCIAL UNION.* **DEM BONES, DEM BONES... ANSWERS:** *1. THIGH; 2. BREAST; 3. HAND; 4. ARM; 5. COLLAR; 7. MIDDLE EAR; 8. ARM; 9. FOOT; 10. SHOULDER.*

HISTOIRE NATURELLE

OK, Natural History!

1. If an animal is arboreal, where does it live?

2. What is an ammonite?

3. Man, lady, soldier, fog and monkey are all types of what flowering plant?

4. What species of animal has the longest tongue?

5. What tree's name also means to yearn for something?

6. What rodent is known scientifically as rattus rattus ?

7. What national park in the US is famous for bears, bison and geysers?

8. What is a cottonmouth?   A) A lamb   B) A weevil   C) A snake

9. By what name is a baby hedgehog known?

10. What amphibian was once believed to be able to live in fire?

ODD ONE OUT

But which one?

COME ON YOU ....

Which football clubs have the following nicknames?

1. RED DEVILS; 2. SAINTS; 3. THE GAS; 4. COTTAGERS
5. RAILWAYMEN; 6. FOXES; 7. POTTERS 8. HORNETS;
9. SEAGULLS; 10. CHERRIES.

HISTOIRE NATURELLE ANSWERS: *1. FULLY OR PARTLY IN TREES;*
2. A FOSSIL; 3. ORCHIDS; 4. GIRAFFE; 5. PINE; 6. BLACK RAT;
7. YELLOWSTONE; 8. C) A SNAKE; 9. A HOGLET; 10. A
SALAMANDER. **ODD ONE OUT ANSWER:** *A (upside down right).*
COME ON YOU ..... ANSWERS: *1. MANCHESTER UNITED;*
2. SOUTHAMPTON; 3. BRISTOL ROVERS; 4. FULHAM; 5. CREWE
ALEXANDRA; 6. LEICESTER CITY; 7. STOKE CITY; 8. WATFORD;
9. BRIGHTON & HOVE ALBION; 10. AFC BOURNEMOUTH.

CRESCENDO

Value of points per question rises as the round progresses

1. **1 POINT.** Cumberland is famous for which meat dish?
A) Bacon   B) Deep fried Mars Bars   C) Sausages

2. **2 POINTS.** Which philosopher coined the term 'I think, therefore I am'
A) Plato   B) Descartes   C) Socrates

3. **3 POINTS.** At the siege of Mafeking who led the British forces?
A) Robert Baden-Powell   B) Colonel B.T. Mahon   C) Louis Mountbatten

4. **4 POINTS.** Casterly Rock is the ancestral home of which family in *Game of Thrones*? A) The Starks   B) The Tully's   C) The Lannisters

5. **5 POINTS.** Pisces and Scorpio are 2 of the water signs. Name the third.
A) Aquarius   B) Cancer   C) Leo

6. **6 POINTS.** How many novels did the Bronte sisters write in total?
A) 9   B) 7   C) 8

7. **7 POINTS.** The Plaka is the oldest quarter of which city?
A) Athens   B) Prague   C) Rome

8. **8 POINTS.** What in America is the Palmetto state?
A) Florida   B) Louisiana   C) South Carolina

9. **9 POINTS.** Julius Caesar said 'The die is cast' after crossing which river?
A) Danube   B) Rubicon   C) Tiber

10. **10 POINTS.** Timber selected from how many fully grown oak trees were needed to build a large 3 deck Royal Navy battleship in the 18th century?
A) 500   B) 1,500   C) 3,500

(UN)FAMILIAR FACES

Who are these celebrities?

A.   **B.**   **C.**   **D.**   **E.**

CRESCENDO ANSWERS: 1. C) SAUSAGES; 2. B) DESCARTES; 3. ROBERT BADEN-POWELL; 4. THE LANNISTERS; 5. B) CANCER; 6. B) 7; 8. C) SOUTH CAROLINA; 9. B) RUBICON; 10. C) 3,500. (UN)FAMILIAR CELEBRITIES ANSWERS: A) DAWN FRENCH; B) NICHOLAS LYNDHURST; C) PAUL McCARTNEY; D) RITA ORA; E) ED SHEERAN.

THE PURSUIT!

General Trivia Questions

1. A nocturne is usually played on what musical instrument?

2. What's the more common title for Edvard Munch's painting The Cry?

3. What male names are used in the NATO phonetic alphabet?

4. What road surface material patented in 1902 was named after a Scottish inventor?

5. In 2017, aerialist Erendira Wallenda set a record by dangling 300 feet from a helicopter hovering over the Niagara Falls by her what?
A) Teeth   B) Thumbs   C) Knicker elastic

6. Forget-me-not flowers are most commonly what colour?

7. Who was top goal scorer for Wales at Euro 2016?

8. What is three-fifths of 75?

9. From which country does Halloumi cheese originate?

10. John Travolta, Kirstie Alley and Tom Cruise are famous followers of what religious movement?

11. What name is given to the sound hole of a violin?

12. Which newspaper coined the word 'suffragette' in 1906?

13. Traditionally, sailors would get a tattoo of what bird after travelling over 5,000 nautical miles?

14. What is the name of the Scottish town that declares itself 'The Malt Whisky Capital of the World'?   A) Rufftown   B) Dufftown   C) Cufftown

15. Which organ in the body cleanses the blood of bacteria and viruses?

16. Who holds the Guinness world record for the longest novel ever written?

17. Braga is a city in which European country

18. Lyrics. Which song opens with these words – "Hell is gone and heaven's here. There's nothing left for you to fear"?

19. Which number in Bingo is often referred to as Gandhi's breakfast?

20. The Thursday Murder Club and The Man Who Died Twice are novels by which author?

THE PURSUIT ANSWERS: 1. PIANO; 2. THE SCREAM; 3. 5 - CHARLIE, MIKE, OSCAR, ROMEO, VICTOR; 4. TARMACADAM; 5. A) TEETH; 6. BLUE; 7. GARETH BALE; 8. 45; 9. CYPRUS; 10. SCIENTOLOGY; 11. F HOLE; 12. DAILY MAIL; 13. SWALLOW; 14. B) DUFFTOWN; 15. SPLEEN; 16. MARCEL PROUST; 17. PORTUGAL; 18. LET ME ENTERTAIN YOU BY ROBBIE WILLIAMS; 19. 80; 20. RICHARD OSMAN.

THE NAMING GAME

Name these celebrities and find the a link between them!

WHAT YEAR WAS THAT?

The quicker you guess when all the events occurred, the more points you get!

1. **5 points.** Cecil Day-Lewis became the Poet Laureate.

2. **4 points.** Prescription charges re-introduced at 2s 6d by Labour government.

3. **3 points.** Alec Rose sailed around the world.

2. **2 points.** Robert Kennedy and Martin Luther King are both assassinated.

5. **1 point**. Manchester United win the European Cup.

THE NAMING GAME ANSWERS: *1. E.L. JAMES; 2. JESSE JAMES; 3. JAMES BLUNT; 4. JAMES; 5. P.D. JAMES; 6. JAMES (JIMMY) GREAVES; 7. ETTA JAMES; 8. JAMES EARL JONES; 9. JAMES CORDEN; 10. JAMES ANDERSON. THE LINK IS THE NAME JAMES.* **WHAT YEAR WAS THAT? ANSWER:** *1968.*

THIS AND THAT!

General Trivia

1. Complete this sequence : C W G C L H A L A …

2. In *Only Fools and Horses*, Trigger claims to have used the same broom for 20 years….even though it has had how many new heads and handles?

3. Who is the young female British tennis star who won the US Open without losing a set in 2021?

4. Eton Mess is a popular dessert of broken meringue, whipped cream and which fruit?

5. What classic chess opening is an attempt by White to sacrifice a pawn in order to gain control of the centre squares?

6. On which country's national flag is there an navy blue emblem known as the Ashoka Chakra, a wheel with 24 spokes?

7. The largest animal known to have ever existed is Balenoptera Musculus. By what name is it more familiarly known?

8. What 2007 film starring Tommy Lee Jones and Javier Bardem was based on a novel by Cormac McCarthy, the title is the first line of a poem *Sailing to Byzantium* by W. B. Yeats?

9. A celebration of Christmas, by the singing of Carols, is traditionally shown on BBC2 each Christmas Eve, from the Chapel of which Cambridge college?

10. True or False? In 1988 a bookseller from Gloucestershire paid £3,575 for a single lock of Lord Nelson's hair.

WHERE IN THE WORLD?

The quicker you get it right, the more points you score!

1. **5 POINTS.** I am a tourist attraction in the US.

2. **4 POINTS.** I have been protected since 1919.

3. **3 POINTS.** I am located on the Kaibab Plateau.

4. **2 POINTS.** The Colorado River runs through me.

5. **1 POINT.** I am 277 miles long.

THIS AND THAT ANSWERS: *1. B (for Beatrice, the line of succession to the throne); 2.17 NEW HEADS AND 14 NEW HANDLES; 3. EMMA RADUCANU; 4.STRAWBERRIES; 5. QUEEN'S GAMBIT; 6. INDIA; 7. BLUE WHALE; 8. NO COUNTRY FOR OLD MEN; 9. KING'S; 10. TRUE.*
WHERE IN THE WORLD ANSWER: *THE GRAND CANYON.*

A WALK IN THE PARK

How well do you know the National parks of the UK and the World?

1. How many National Parks are there in Scotland?
2. The Kruger National Park, one of the largest game reserves in Africa, is to be found in which country?
3. Fiordland National Park is the largest national park in which country?
4. Which is England's newest national park, becoming operational in 2011?
5. Hadrian's Wall crosses which national park?
6. The Serengeti National Park is in which African country?
7. Which American National Park is home to the General Sherman tree, the largest tree on Earth?
8. Which national park became the United Kingdom's first in 1951?
9. The first 10 UK national parks were opened in which 20th century decade?
10. How many national parks are there in Wales?

SEQUENTIAL SEARCH

The first letter of each answer follows that of the previous answer alphabetically. You need to work out what the first letter used is though!

1. A Christmas film from 1946, starring James Stewart, that is still popular.
2. *Ain't No Doubt* was a Number 3 hit for which star of *Auf Wiedersehen, Pet*?
3. Name the largest landlocked country in the world (and 9th largest)?
4. The surname of H.E. Bates family written about in the Darling Buds of May.
5. Rebecca Adlington and Ed Davey were born in which Nottinghamshire town?
6. Which small Arctic whale has a long, straight tusk originating from its teeth?
7. Which chemical element is number 8 on the periodic table?
8. Which Posh football club's home ground is London Road Stadium?
9. What is the code word for Q in the phonetic alphabet?
10. Who drives the Crimson Haybailer in the *Wacky Races*?

 **TRIVIAtime**

Which famous American novelist said - "If you tell the truth, you don't have to remember anything."

A WALK IN THE PARK ANSWERS: 1. 2 (Loch Lomond and The Trossachs and the Cairngorms; 2. SOUTH AFRICA; 3. NEW ZEALAND; 4. THE SOUTH DOWNS; 5. NORTHUMBERLAND; 6. TANZANIA; 7.SEQUOIA (CALIFORNIA); 8.THE PEAK DISTRICT; 9. 1950s; 10. 3 (Snowdonia, Pembrokeshire Coast & 2. JIMMY NAIL; 3. KAZAKHSTAN; 4. LARKINS; 5. MANSFIELD; 6. NARWHAL; 7. OXYGEN; 8. PETERBOROUGH UNITED; 9. QUEBEC; 10. RED MAX.
TRIVIAtime ANSWER: MARK TWAIN.

WEATHER REPORT

How much do you know about the weather?

1. The 11th century Bayeux Tapestry shows a man installing a rooster weather vane on which London place of worship?

2. What name is given for the amount of water vapour present in the air?

3. Which BBC weatherman's 1987 prediction that the Great Storm was a false alarm is still remembered as a classic TV gaffe?

4. What measurement scale is used to determine wind speed?

5. The strong winds caused by high pressure over the Mohave Desert in California are known as what?

6. What temperature is the same on both Celsius and Fahrenheit scales?

7. A tropical storm in the region of the Indian or western Pacific oceans is commonly called what?

8. What does a barometer measure?

9. What is a fear of snow called?

10. Name the following shipping forecast weather area named after an island in the Bristol Channel?

TRUE OR FALSE

50% chance of getting these right!

1. Spaghetto is the singular form of the word spaghetti.

2. Venezuela is the location of the world's highest waterfall.

3. The longest river in the world is the Amazon.

4. The moon is wider than Australia.

5. In 19th century Britain, if you tried and failed to commit suicide you were hung!

6. When going out of the cave, the bats always turn right.

7. Nepal is the only country in the world without a rectangular flag.

8. Prince Harry is taller than Prince William

9. We reach our lowest ebb at 2.16pm each day.

10. Madonna was fired by Dunkin' Donuts for squirting jam at a customer.

WEATHER REPORT ANSWERS: *1. WESTMINSTER ABBEY; 2. HUMIDITY; 3. MICHAEL FISH; 4. BEAUFORT SCALE; 5. SANTA ANA WINDS; 6. 40°C/40°F; 7. TYPHOON; 8. ATMOSPHERIC PRESSURE; 9. CHIONOPHOBIA; 10. LUNDY.*
TRUE OR FALSE? ANSWERS: *1. TRUE; 2. TRUE; 3. FALSE (the Nile); 4. FALSE (The moon diameter 3400k, Australia over 4000k); 5. TRUE; 6. FALSE (Always turn right); 7. TRUE; 8. FALSE (William 1.91m, Harry 1.86m); 9. TRUE; 10. TRUE.*

ROUND ROBIN

The last letter of the first answer is the first letter of the second answer and so on. The last letter of answer 10 is also the first letter of answer 1 to complete the circle

1. The name of the London Marathon co-founder with Chris Brasher in 1981.

2. Which anthropomorphic animal character lives in Jellystone Park and has a liking for picnic baskets?

3. The ….. Is a poem by Edgar Allen Poe which starts, 'Once upon a midnight dreary….'

4. A western US state in which 75% of the population live in Clark County.

5. A village on the River Severn with a ferry crossing for hundreds of years prior to the Severn Bridge opening in 1966. Famously used by Bob Dylan.

6. The home of Harlequins RFC,The Stoop, is located in which affluent town?

7. Mrs…… is a character in Sheridan's *The Rivals*, who gets her words all muddled up.

8. A tropical plant with an edible fruit and the most economically significant plant in the family Bromeliaceae. Tinned in chunks or rings.

9. An examination of the body using a camera held on to a flexible tube.

10. A song written by Paul McCartney, one of the most recorded songs in pop music history. It is also the title of a successful 2019 Danny Boyle film.

The writer of Robinson Crusoe, Daniel Defoe, visited Aust Ferry in the 18th Century but decided not to make the crossing there because it was so dangerous. "When we came to Aust, the hither side of the Passage, the sea was so broad, the fame of the Bore of the tide so formidable, the wind also made the water so rough, and which was worse, the boats to carry over both man and horse appear'd (as I have said above) so very mean, that in short none of us car'd to venture: So we came back, and resolv'd to keep on the road to Gloucester."

The ferry service was expanded in 1934. The Severn Queen could take 17 cars at a time. But the huge tidal range of the Severn made the timetable notoriously unreliable.

The first Severn Bridge is actually two bridges, a bridge across the Severn linked to a bridge across the River Wye. Only the bridge across the Wye links England to Wales as Beachley (at the end of the first span) is still in England!

ROUND ROBIN ANSWERS: *1. JOHN DISLEY; 2. YOGI BEAR; 3. RAVEN; 4. NEVADA; 5. AUST; 6. TWICKENHAM; 7. MALAPROP; 8. PINEAPPLE; 9. ENDOSCOPY; 10. YESTERDAY.*

WHEN E.T. MET DRACULA!

Reworked film pictures. Can you guess the 10 pairs of movies featured in the pics?

WHEN E.T. MET DRACULA ANSWERS: *1. THE SOUND OF MUSIC & DRIVING MISS DAISY; 2. RAIDERS OF THE LOST ARK & E.T.; 3. CHARIOTS OF FIRE & FORREST GUMP; 4. SINGIN' IN THE RAIN & SUMMER HOLIDAY; 5. ZULU & AIRPLANE!; 6. MURDER AHOY AND DR. NO; 7. THE SILENCE OF THE LAMBS & NATIONAL LAMPOONS CHRISTMAS VACATION; 8. THE PINK PANTHER STRIKES AGAIN & THE ITALIAN JOB; 9. BACK TO THE FUTURE & THE BUDDY HOLLY STORY; 10. THE WIZARD OF OZ & THE EXORCIST.*

EUROPEAN EXCURSION

9 questions to answer then find the link for number 10

1. In which country was Hamlet a prince?
2. The Van Gogh museum is located in which country?
3. Name the country famous for chocolate, waffles, beer and Hercule Poirot.
4. Which early commercial radio station featured The Ovaltineys and Leslie Welch, the memory man, on 208 on Sunday evenings?
5. Liberty, Equality and Fraternity is the translated motto of what country?
6. Monte Rosa is the highest mountain in which country?
7. Hitler was born on 28 April 1889 in the town of Braunau am Inn, in which country?
8. Which country became independent on 1 January 1993?
9. Ludwig Zamantof created Esperanto. In which country was he born?
10. What links the 9 answers?

FOOTBALL ANAGRAMS

English Football Clubs

1. I'M MARCHING BY IT

2. STOIC TRILBY

3. RIVER ROT SLOBS

4. URINE DETACHMENTS

5. ERROR FORGET SEVENS

6. TO THE POSH TANTRUM

7. REALLY GOT HUMPY

8. SUDDEN ELITE

9. WET DENSE LUNATIC

10. QUEER SPANKERS RANG

EUROPEAN EXCURSION ANSWERS: 1. DENMARK; 2. NETHERLANDS; 3. BELGIUM; 4. LUXEMBOURG; 5. FRANCE; 6. SWITZERLAND; 7. AUSTRIA; 8. CZECH REPUBLIC; 9. POLAND; 10. THEY ALL SHARE A BORDER WITH GERMANY. FOOTBALL ANAGRAMS ANSWERS: 1. BIRMINGHAM CITY; 2. BRISTOL CITY; 3. BRISTOL ROVERS; 4. MANCHESTER UNITED; 5. FOREST GREEN ROVERS; 6. TOTTENHAM HOTSPUR; 7. PLYMOUTH ARGYLE; 8. LEEDS UNITED; 9. NEWCASTLE UNITED; 10. QUEENS PARK RANGERS.

ALL KINDS OF EVERYTHING
A variety of teasers

1. Complete the sequence: 11,25,19, 17, 24, 24, 15, 24, 26, ..

2. True or False? The potato belongs to the same family as deadly nightshade.

3. What are: Moselle, Fleet, Stamford Brook and Tyburn?

4. And, what are: Abondance, Reblochon and Livarot?

5. Who is known as Mikulas in Hungary and Viejo Pascuero in Chile?

6. Who played Prince Florizel in Cinderella at Windsor Castle in 1941?

7. What does Leonardo Di Caprio have a phobia about?
A) Doorknobs   B) Cracks in the pavement   C) Graveyards

8. In 2019, Harry Ramsden's fish and chip shop empire was bought by rival company Deep Blue Restaurants. True or False?

9. Isca Dumnonioruman was originally a Roman legionary fortress. Which city now occupies the site?

10. In 2006, which famous football club moved to a new stadium just a 12 minute walk away from their long established home ground?

11. What3words is a geocode system for identifying a location with a resolution of about 3 metres. Which sporting venue will you fin d at: mostly.proper.petty?

12. A man rode out of town on Sunday, he stayed a whole night at a hotel and rode back to town the next day on Sunday. How is this possible?

13. What begins with an "e" and usually only contains one letter?

14. What number is missing from the sequence: 1, 8, 27, 64, ?, 216?

15. A red house has four walls. All the walls are red and are facing south, and a bear is circling the house. There's also a red storage container outside. What colour is the bear?

ALL KINDS OF EVERYTHING ANSWERS: 1. 26 (UK POSITIONS IN THE 10 EUROVISION SONG CONTESTS UP TO 2021); 2. TRUE; 3. SUBTERRANEAN RIVERS OF LONDON; 4. FRENCH CHEESES; 5. FATHER CHRISTMAS; 6. THE QUEEN; 7. B) CRACKS IN THE PAVEMENT; 8. TRUE; 9. EXETER; 10. ARSENAL; 11. LORDS CRICKET GROUND; 12.HIS HORSE WAS CALLED SUNDAY; 13. AN ENVELOPE; 14.125 (THEY'RE CUBES, FROM 1 TO 6); 15. WHITE (The house must be on the north pole for all the walls to face south and the only bears in the north pole region are polar bears).

GONE BUT NOT FORGOTTEN

So many stars passed in 2021. Here are 31 of them! How many can you name? May they all R.I.P.

GONE BUT NOT FORGOTTEN ANSWERS: 1. TREVOR PEACOCK; 2. CAPTAIN SIR TOM MOORE; 3. PRINCE PHILIP; 4. JOHN CHALLIS; 5. MARY WILSON; 6. CHRIS BARBER; 7. SARAH HARDING; 8.JIMMY GREAVES; 9. IAN ST. JOHN;10. UNA STUBBS; 11. CHARLIE WATTS; 12. NICOLA PAGETT; 13. SEAN LOCK; 14. HELEN McGRORY; 15.CHRISTOPHER PLUMMER; 16. LES McKEOWN; 17. MARVELOUS MARVIN HAGLER; 18. MURRAY WALKER; 19. GERRY MARSDEN; 20. DAVE EGERTON; 21. PAUL RITTER; 22. JOHNNY BRIGGS; 23. ALAN LANCASTER; 24. TOM O'CONNOR; 25. MICHAEL COLLINS; 26. FRANK WORTHINGTON; 27. DON EVERLY; 28. ROBERT FYFE; 29. ROGER HUNT; 30. HILTON VALENTINE; 31. CLIVE SINCLAIR.

HICKORY DICKORY DOCK
Rodents of all kinds!

1. Rodents breed very swiftly, so why have they not overrun the Earth?

2. How many teeth do rodents have?
A) 2 upper, 2 lower   B) 3 upper, 3 lower   C) 4 upper, 4 lower

3. Are all rodents vegetarians?
A) Yes   B) No they eat flesh   C) Most (except squirrels)

4. Many rodents have cheek pouches. To prevent inedible material entering their stomach. True or false?

5. What North American 'dog' is a rodent?

6. Which rodents can be found on nearly every continent?
A) Porcupines   B) Rats and mice   C) Moles

7. What is the name of the pet mouse in the film, *The Green Mile*?

8. What rodents of the genus *Dipodomys*, are native to arid areas of western North America and can leap 7 feet (2.13 metres)?

9. What is a group of prairie dogs called?

10. Who is the deadliest enemy of rodents?
A) Humans   B) Birds of prey   C) Predatory animals

CUTE CREATURES
Name these animals

HICKORY DICKORY DOCK ANSWERS: *1. RODENTS ARE THE PREY OF ALMOST ALL FLESH-EATING ANIMALS; 2. A) 2 UPPER, 2 LOWER; 3. C) MOST (EXCEPT SQUIRRELS); 4. FALSE (FOR CARRYING FOOD); 5. PRAIRIE DOG; 6. B) RATS AND MICE; 7. MR. JINGLES; 8. KANGAROO RATS; 9. A TOWN; 10. A) HUMANS.*
CUTE CREATURES ANSWERS: *A) MEERKAT; B) PUFFIN; C) ALPACA; D) LEMUR.*

WATCHING THE DETECTIVES

Marry up the TV detectives with their creators

DETECTIVE	CHARACTER CREATOR
1. JANE MARPLE	A. GEORGES SIMENON
2. FATHER BROWN	B. IAN RANKIN
3. DCI REG WEXFORD	C. SALLY WAINWRIGHT
4. DS ROY GRACE	D. PETER ROBINSON
5. DCI ALAN BANKS	E. AGATHA CHRISTIE
6. DI ENDEAVOUR MORSE	F. G.K. CHESTERTON
7. D/SUPT JANE TENNISON	G. RUTH RENDELL
8. SHERLOCK HOLMES	H. W.J. BURLEY
9. CMDR ADAM DALGLIESH	I. ANN CLEEVES
10. DCI RODERICK ALLEYN	J. PETER JAMES
11. DCI VERA STANHOPE	K. NGAIO MARSH
12. DI JACK FROST	L. LYNDA LA PLANTE
13. DI ALEC HARDY	M. COLIN DEXTER
14. DCI JOHN LUTHER	N. JED MERCURIO
15. DCI JANINE LEWIS	P. ARTHUR CONAN DOYLE
16. DCS CHRISTOPHER FOYLE	Q. P.D. JAMES
17. DI GEORDIE KEATING	R. R.D. WINGFIELD
18. DI GEORGE GENTLY	S. CHRIS CHIBNALL
19. D/SUPT TED HASTINGS	T. CAROLINE GRAHAM
20. DC JANET SCOTT	U. CATH STAINCLIFFE
21. D/SUPT CHARLES WYCLIFFE	V. ANTHONY HOROWITZ
22. CI JULES MAIGRET	W. JAMES RUNCIE
23. DCI TOM BARNABY	X. ALAN HUNTER
24. DI JOHN REBUS	Y. ROBERT THOROGOOD
25. DI RICHARD POOLE	Z. NEIL CROSS

WATCHING THE DETECTIVES ANSWERS: *1E; 2F; 3G; 4J; 5D; 6M; 7L; 8P; 9Q; 10K; 11I; 12R; 13S; 14Z; 15U; 16V; 17W; 18X; 19N; 20C; 21H; 22A; 23T; 24B; 25Y.*

TOPICAL TEST
Questions on recent history

1. At what time in the UK did Brexit fully come into force on 31 December 2020?

2. Which country changed their national anthem lyrics to reflect the spirit of unity and the indigenous population?

3. Who was the long-serving conservative MP brutally murdered whilst conducting a constituency surgery in Leigh-on-Sea on 15 October 2021?

4. Who was voted the 'Most admired man in America' for 2020?

5. Climate protest group Insulate Britain caused disruption to major roads during 2021. What is Insulate Britain's aim?

6. What aid did the queen use in public for the first time in October 2021?

7. Why was PC Chris Dwyer, a police constable from West Yorkshire, sacked in October 2021?

8. After Lockdown, what did the government tell GPs to do?

9. What is the name of the James Bond film released in 2021

10. Which famous London building celebrated its 150th anniversary in 2021?

11. The 2021 UN Climate Change Conference took place in which British city?

12. Express the year 2021 in roman numerals?

13. NASA launched the James Webb Space Telescope, a successor to which telescope?

14. The UK finished bottom with 'No Points' in the 2021 Eurovision Song Contest. Where was it held?

15. Which toy company announced it wanted to remove gender stereotypes from its products?

 **TRIVIAtime**

In 2021 the Royal Mint confirmed that it has worked with the Royal Palace to design some special coins to tell us more about which monarch?

IT'S A PUPPET!

Name these famous puppets

IT'S A PUPPET ANSWERS: 1. SOOTY; 2. BASIL BRUSH; 3. BILL AND BEN; 4. SOOTY; 5. FOZZIE BEAR; 6. PINOCCHIO; 7. LADY PENELOPE; 8. JOEY (War Horse); 9. WALTER; 10. ORVILLE.

A FINAL TEASER

Use the picture clues to identify a major celebrity

THE FINAL COUNTDOWN

Last round. Hope you have enjoyed the challenges in this book

1. *The Final Countdown* reached number 1 in the UK in 1986. Who were the Swedish hit-makers?

2. In which Spanish city was the dish Paella invented?

3. What links Europe's highest mountain and a luxury brand of pens?

4. What is the oldest remaining palace in London?

5. How long is the course for the University Boat Race on the River Thames?

6. Who was the last Scottish player to win The Open?

7. What cartoon character's given names are officially Bartholomew JoJo?

8. Which Tolstoy novel begins, 'All happy families are alike, each unhappy in its own way'?

9. Banksy is most associated with which city?

10. Finally, what is the longest words that can make from **COUNTDOWN**?

THE FINAL COUNTDOWN ANSWERS; *1. EUROPE; 2. VALENCIA; 3. MONT BLANC; 4. HAMPTON COURT PALACE; 5. 4.2 MILES (6.8 km); 6. PAUL LAWRIE; 7. BART SIMPSON; 8. ANNA KARENINA; 9. BRISTOL; 10. 7 LETTER WORDS – CUTDOWN, WOODCUT, NUTWOOD.*

THE INQUIZITORS
Some action shots of Mike, Rob and Mo

Mike sound check at Celtic Manor

Rob at the DoubleTree Hilton

Mo check at Ashton Gate

An unusual Inquizitors venue -
The National Museum of Wales, Cardiff

A matter of opinion!

Bigger events need more scorers
like Mandy & Wayne!

We have done many quizzes for
Steve & Carole for Bristol
Haematology & Oncology Centre

One of many happy teams to
receive Inquizitors certificates

Ready for action at Nailsworth

Our original stand sponsored
by Avon Exhibitions

Mo and Rob hard at work

Mike and Rob in full flow at Bristol City

More happy winners
at Bowood Hotel

Mo with Sam - a future Inquizitor!

The Inquizitors are grateful to all the people who have helped at many of the big quiz events

Printed in Great Britain
by Amazon

69526163R00071